TANKS
ON THE SOMME

TANKS
ON THE SOMME
FROM MORVAL TO BEAUMONT HAMEL

TREVOR PIDGEON

FOREWORD BY
DAVID FLETCHER

Pen & Sword
MILITARY

First published in Great Britain in 2010 by
Pen & Sword Military
an imprint of
Pen & Sword Books Ltd
47 Church Street
Barnsley
South Yorkshire
S70 2AS

ISBN 978 1 84884 253 3

A CIP catalogue record for this book is available from the British Library

Printed and bound in England by
the MPG Books Group

Pen & Sword Books Ltd incorporates the Imprints of Pen & Sword Aviation,
Pen & Sword Maritime, Pen & Sword Military, Wharncliffe Local History,
Pen and Sword Select, Pen and Sword Military Classics, Leo Cooper,
Remember When, Seaforth Publishing and Frontline Publishing.

For a complete list of Pen & Sword titles please contact
PEN & SWORD BOOKS LIMITED
47 Church Street, Barnsley, South Yorkshire, S70 2AS, England
E-mail: enquiries@pen-and-sword.co.uk
Website: www.pen-and-sword.co.uk

CONTENTS

LIST OF MAPS

Notes on the Maps and Illustrations

Sadly, Trevor Pidgeon passed away early in 2008 before he had completed the map and illustration sections of this book. When he realised that he would be unable to do so he asked if I would be able to do them for him. This I have done and trust that Trevor would have been happy with the end result.

The illustrations are all ones selected or produced by Trevor with captions based on his notes.

For the maps I have produced a set of trench maps using Trevor's text. It was not always possible to find a published trench map which corresponded exactly with the date of the tank action so, in several cases, I have had to either introduce trench lines from other maps or to accentuate poorly defined lines using dotted or dashed lines respectively. In some instances Trevor gives trench map references to locations at some distance from the sites of the tank actions and consequently these are not always shown on the accompanying maps. In producing these maps I am most grateful to Memory-Map Inc. for permission to use and reproduce their maps and to Guy Smith for guidance in manipulation of the systems.

In three cases, numbers 1, 9 and 11, I have produced my own sketch maps to indicate the general geography of the area of operations. Where chapters include a Field Guide, the numbers of the required French Institut Géographique National 'Blue Series' maps have been included.

Trench maps were divided into rectangles, identified by letters, and each of these was subdivided into squares, identified by numbers. Thus on map 2 the rectangles M, N, S and T are shown. Ginchy is located in rectangle T, square 13.

The squares were further subdivided into squares a, b, c and d. Thus the crossroads in Ginchy can be found in T.13.d and Arrow Head Copse in S.30.b. For even greater accuracy the sides of each small square were divided into ten, reading *along* and then *up* to find a particular point. Thus the Ginchy crossroads are at T.13.d.8.5. and Arrow Head Copse at S.30.b.3.3.

Graham Keech
Banstead, 2009

Acknowledgements

I am grateful to all those friends who gave me the benefit of their time and expertise from the very moment that I began to write this book.

In particular I have to thank David Fletcher of the Tank Museum at Bovington, who originally asked me to undertake this work of chronicling what he called the 'Dark Ages' of early tank history. His own encyclopaedic knowledge of mechanised armour is recognised worldwide, as is his readiness to share this with others.

I must also thank Guy Smith for his friendship, patience and understanding when I sought his help with my (thankfully occasional) computer problems, and for explaining to me the mysteries of digitised mapping and the application of GPS to First World War history.

As ever, the late Jean Verdel of Miraumont was a source of much background detail. He was always ready to advise or to seek the advice of others on my behalf on whatever problem I put to him.

Sadly, Monty Rossiter, a 'tankie' from as far back as 1934, died before this book was completed, but during his lifetime he was a good friend and support, offering helpful comment whenever I drew on his wide knowledge and sound judgement.

And thanks, too, to Miss Patricia White, who read the book in draft to rid it of its undoubted errors of spelling, grammar and style.

Finally, I must thank my wife Marion, for her encouragement, support and willingness to keep me supplied with coffee whenever the need arose.

Trevor Pidgeon
Cobham

As a post-script may I commend to the reader the following books, all of which are well researched, readily available and inexpensive guides to the fighting. They may not dwell long on the tank aspects of each battle but otherwise they provide a valuable contribution to the *Battleground Europe* series published by Pen & Sword Ltd of Barnsley. Nigel Cave: *Beaumont-Hamel*; Nigel Cave and Jack Horsfall: *Serre*; Michael Stedman: *Thiepval*; Graham Keech: *Pozières*; Paul Reed: *Courcelette*; Michael Renshaw: *Beaucourt*; Jack Sheldon: *The Germans at Thiepval*, and *The Germans at Beaumont-Hamel*.

Foreword

Anyone who knew Trevor Pidgeon would be able to tell you that his approach to research and writing was meticulous - not just in collating material from dusty archives but in walking the ground, flying over it and following up every lead, however obscure it might seem to be. The result, *The Tanks at Flers*, is there for all to see.

Why the subject appealed to him so strongly is not too clear. Trevor put it down to his own military service and his familiarity with the battlefield but I suspect it had as much to do with an innate curiosity and determination to tell a story which had long been overlooked. You will see from the Acknowledgements that he blamed me for this latest title. That is probably true; I knew the task needed doing and I could not think of anyone better fitted to do it. What I did not know, of course, is that he would not live to see it published. His wise choice of Graham Keech to see it through to publication is another indication of how astute he was.

This, however, is not the end of the story by any means. From these faltering beginnings the tanks went on to do much more but it was not plain sailing. The battles around Arras in April 1917, followed by the long, wet summer in the Salient, nearly saw the tank abandoned for the duration; yet at Cambrai, that November, the tank's potential shone through in a new light. And 1918, once the German offensive had been halted in its tracks, brought success upon success. At present we are passing through a period when many of our more revered historians are playing down the significance of the tank in favour of other arms, but this was not how it was seen at the time. One only has to look at the proposed production figures for 1919 to realise that.

Trevor avoided academic controversy; he stuck to the facts and told a story clearly. But I think he realised something that tends to get overlooked. No matter what it actually achieved on the battlefield, it was a remarkable statement of the British will to win by bending innovation and technical skill to the war effort.

David Fletcher
The Tank Museum
Bovington
April 2009

Preface

In writing this book I have drawn on contemporary sources, battle orders, reports and eye-witness accounts to describe the actions of Britain's Mark I tanks – the world's first – during the later phases of the Battle of the Somme in 1916. I have already described[1] their actions on 15 September of that year, when they made their initial appearance on the battlefield, and also on the 16th, when a few of the surviving machines were employed on small-scale operations in the 'driblets' or 'penny-packets' which their designers and advocates at home had warned against from the outset. Here I deal with their actions – still in penny-packets – from late September to mid-November, when the Somme campaign drew to a close.

I trust the reader will forgive me for choosing not to describe in detail the actions of other arms in these operations – infantry and artillery especially – despite the fact that they played a far greater role in the struggle than did the new 'landships'. There is already an abundance of literature on the Somme campaign in general and a multitude of books on individual divisions, regiments, operations and indeed on individual soldiers, all of which the reader will find of interest and value in understanding the fighting. Britain's *Official History of the War* (Military Operations, France and Belgium, 1916, part 2), is available in re-print from many booksellers and public libraries and provides a readable, general account despite its rather dry style. I have unashamedly used this throughout as a convenient source of comment on the non-tank aspects of the story. In addition, there are the books listed in my Acknowledgements.

For my own part, as I say, I have chosen to concentrate on the work of the tanks and their crews because I believe that more should be done to accord them the honoured place they deserve in our nation's history. This is an attempt to record for the reader the achievements and the failures, the successes and disappointments of the men who first took these machines into battle, so that their courage and devotion to duty will not be overlooked by history. It may be that the story will appeal more to the tank enthusiast than it will to the general reader, but even he or she may find it of interest to follow in the path of these machines and in doing so to get to know some corners of

---

[1] See the author's *The Tanks at Flers* (ISBN 0952517523), published by Fairmile Books (1995).

the battlefields not often visited by tourists and some corners of our history almost never described by historians.

For the first tankmen disappointments were plentiful; their machines had to contend not only with the artillery and trenches of the enemy but also with the heavy rain and deep mud which came to characterise this battleground in the autumn and early winter of 1916. Time and again operations were modified, postponed or abandoned because of adverse weather conditions. And when they did go forward the tanks often became 'bellied' in the morass, their tracks gradually grinding their way down into the sponge-like soil until the floor of the hull came into contact with the ground, where it acted as a powerful brake on forward progress.

The reader will see that 'ditching' was frequently the fate of these tanks, but this term is a general one, used to describe any form of stoppage caused by falling into a trench, crashing into a shell hole or even, as occasionally happened, breaking through the roof of an unseen dug-out. 'Ditching' was also applied to a tank that had 'bellied' and been abandoned. The truth is that the Mark I tank was designed at a time (the autumn and winter of 1915) when battlefields showed few of the signs of ploughed-up chaos such as was to be seen everywhere on the Somme a year later. That the machine coped at all with the conditions it encountered is a tribute to the crews who manned it and to its design – a design which lasted with relatively minor modifications throughout the war up to and including the Advance to Victory in 1918.

It is true that these first models suffered also from mechanical breakdowns. The tail-wheels – those aids to steering so characteristic of the Mark I – were vulnerable to damage by enemy shellfire and sometimes when just crossing uneven terrain. In some cases the tank's tracks became loose, while in others they broke because of a lack of lubrication. The gravity fuel feed was unreliable. The 105 hp engine showed itself to be underpowered, especially when the tank had to be extricated after ditching.

But it cannot be denied that the Mark I tank was a success, for where conditions were favourable it fulfilled the role for which it had been created: that of clearing a way for the infantry to advance. The problem was that in the autumn and early winter of 1916 favourable conditions were rare.

In describing the events of that time I have chosen not to follow a strictly chronological order – that is, recounting all actions taking place along the front on one day, followed by all those taking place on the next – for to do so would mean hopping around from one area of conflict to another and thus losing the sequence of developments in each place. I trust the reader will find it a more satisfactory way of following the tanks' progress if I describe each operation in each place from beginning to end. The distinction may not, of course, seem important, especially since most of these actions took place within the space of a single day.

Chapter 1

Background

The Battle of the Somme which opened on 1 July 1916 had several purposes. The first was, of course, to inflict as much damage as possible on the German invader and force him to withdraw from the land that he had seized. A second aim was to draw some of his strength away from the French, who were fighting, at enormous cost, to block his path towards Verdun where he was seeking to 'bleed France white'. A third was mainly political – to demonstrate to the French that Britain was a dependable ally, ready, once its army had been brought up to strength, to shoulder some of the burden which France had borne almost alone for nearly two years. This process was slow, for Britain's small expeditionary force of professional soldiers (reputedly described by the Kaiser as her 'contemptible little army'), most of whom had been trained before the war more as an imperial police force, had now been largely destroyed in fighting during and after the disastrous retreat from Mons in 1914. At first, their replacements, drawn from Britain and the Empire, were all volunteers, men who only a few months before had been civilians engaged in peaceful pursuits, blissfully unaware of the horrors that lay ahead of them. In overall terms they were no match for their continental counterparts, members of professionally trained forces several times larger than Britain's.

When the flow of volunteers began to dry up, Britain copied the continentals and introduced conscription and this, coupled with the arrival of further reinforcements from the Empire, began to redress the balance. The process roughly coincided with the appointment of General Sir Douglas Haig as Commander-in-Chief in succession to Field Marshal Sir John French, whose performance in the post had been widely considered inadequate.

As soon as he took office in December 1915 Haig began to prepare his first major offensive, timed for the summer of 1916. The ground chosen was once more dictated largely by political considerations. Following reorganisation of the lines in 1915, the Somme was now the point of junction between the French and British armies and therefore of symbolic significance to both

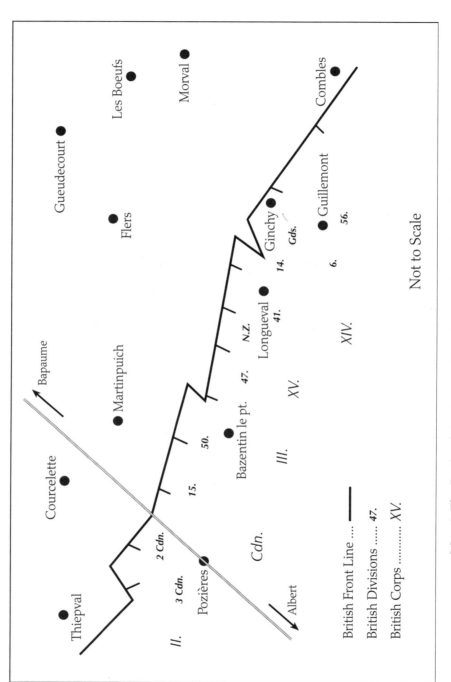

Map 1. The Battle of the Somme: Flers-Courcelette, 15 September 1916.

Thiepval

Courcelette

Bapaume

Gueudecourt

Les Boeufs

Martinpuich

Morval

Flers

3 Cdn.

2 Cdn.

Pozières

15.

50.

Bazentin le pt.

47.

N.Z.

Longueval

41.

Ginchy

14.

Gds.

Combles

Guillemont

56.

6.

II.

Cdn.

III.

XV.

XIV.

Albert

Not to Scale

British Front Line .... ———

British Divisions ...... 47.

British Corps .... XV.

countries. The area had no great strategic value but it was not unsuited to the sort of offensive which the British High Command thought its newly expanded but still partly untrained army could mount.

Haig's plan was ambitious and looked for substantial gains along a front of 14 miles, stretching from Montauban on the right to Gommecourt on the left. Zero hour on 1 July followed a heavy artillery barrage which, alas, failed to destroy the deep defences constructed by the Germans over the preceding months. These defences, coupled with brave, skilled and determined resistance by the Germans, led to horrendous losses among the British, who sustained 57,000 casualties on the first day, one third of them killed. Only on the right was any real progress made.

The following weeks saw a slow and painful advance up towards the top of the ridge crowned by the villages of Pozières and Thiepval. All along the line casualties mounted and it was clear that any further progress would again be costly in killed and wounded.

But Haig had a trump card to play: the tank. Soon after taking up his appointment in December 1915 he had heard about the work being done in England to produce this new weapon of war and immediately welcomed it, calling for its delivery in greater numbers than were thought necessary by some (certainly by the Secretary of State for War, Field Marshal Lord Kitchener, who grudgingly conceded that just *six* should be built) and at an earlier date than the factories at home could produce them. They were not available for the opening of the Somme offensive and only reached France during August and September.

By this time Haig was preparing to resume his offensive, concentrating his efforts in the area between Combles in the east and Courcelette in the west, just beyond the main Albert–Bapaume highway. The ensuing struggle, called thereafter the Battle of Flers-Courcelette, opened on 15 September and was targeted mainly against the villages of Flers and Gueudecourt in the centre, together with Morval, Les Boeufs, Martinpuich and Courcelette on the flanks. More distant targets reflected Haig's ambitions for a major breakthrough against the German positions.

In the event these ambitions were not realised, the tanks aiding the British advance in a number of places but failing to bring about a collapse of the enemy's line. The whole attack involved four corps and ten divisions. On the right stood XIV Corps, with 56th, 6th and Guards Divisions facing Morval and Les Boeufs. In the centre was XV Corps with 14th, 41st and New Zealand Divisions facing Gueudecourt and Flers. On the left, III Corps, with 47th, 50th and 15th Divisions, faced High Wood and Martinpuich, while on the extreme left flank the Canadian Corps attacked with the 2nd Canadian Division facing Courcelette.

Various objectives[1] were assigned to each corps – four in some cases, in others only one. The First Objective was reached almost everywhere, the Fourth not at all.

The tanks had mixed fortunes. Two went well beyond the Third Objective, unsupported by infantry, but both were eventually destroyed. Another went down the High Street of Flers 'with the British Army cheering behind', according to press reports. Others attacked trenches, machine-gun emplacements and strong-points, but some became ditched or simply broke down. Not altogether surprisingly, the day's outcome was interpreted as a success by those infantry where the tanks did well but more harshly by those where they did not.

For his part, Haig thought the tanks had justified his faith in them and promptly despatched his Deputy Chief of Staff to London to argue for a thousand more. In the meantime he drew up plans for using as profitably as he could those machines that had survived the fighting, together with the small numbers that had arrived in France too late to take part in the main battle.

It is the actions of these later machines that we have attempted to describe in this book, being almost the last operations in which Mark I tanks – the world's *first* tanks – took part. Their commanders and crews were no less brave than those who went to war before them or after them and it is fitting that their deeds should be accorded recognition in at least this small corner of military history.

---

[1] The word 'objective' (with a small initial) was often used rather loosely to mean any target which a body of attacking troops was required to reach. It could be a road, a wood or even a minor feature such as a house. More formally, it referred to what might better be termed a 'pause line', one of several lines drawn on the map to indicate where the attackers – a battalion, say, or a corps – were to pause, consolidate, 'mop up' and then reorganise in readiness for the next forward bound. Objectives in this sense were numbered 1, 2, 3, 4, etc, and were often shown on the maps by a colour, normally green, brown, blue and red. In these cases we have made the distinction clear by using capital letters, e.g. First Objective, Second Objective, etc.

Tank Operations:
FOURTH ARMY
(General Sir Henry Rawlinson)

South-east of the Albert–Bapaume road
September–November 1916

Chapter 2

Morval and Les Boeufs:
25–27 September

The resumed offensive here, on the right of the British line, was to open on 25
September. For this attack the Fourth Army commander, General Rawlinson,
had brought up the 5th Division to bolster the strength of XIV Corps, which
had suffered severely on the 15th. The new plan called for the 5th, 6th and
Guards Divisions to launch the main assault on Morval and Les Boeufs, while
56th Division formed a defensive flank on 5th Division's right, facing south-
east towards Combles. The attack by the three first-named divisions was to be
delivered in three stages, each stage mounted in turn against one of three
Objectives – the Green, Brown and Blue Lines – starting respectively at Zero,
Zero plus one hour, and Zero plus two hours. Each Objective was to be
pounded by a 'stationary' barrage placed ahead of the infantry attack but then
lifted as the British advanced towards it behind a 'creeping' barrage, this
process being repeated at the next Objective.

At a conference held on 19 September, Rawlinson outlined to all his Corps
Commanders some of his ideas for the attack, including the use of tanks:

> [*Each*] Corps will hold as many tanks as possible for the attack. They
> should, where possible, be placed in covered positions from which they
> can be brought up to assist in the capture of the villages of Gueudecourt,
> Les Boeufs and Morval after the troops have reached the Brown Line, but
> they should not be moved across the open in daylight to the attack of the
> Green and Brown Lines.

So the tanks were to be used only after the infantry had gone well forward and
had breached the First Objective and reached the Second. In saying this,
Rawlinson clearly had in mind the fate of the two tanks destroyed by shell-fire
on the 15th between Flers and Gueudecourt, and that of three more knocked
out in the same area on the 16th. All of these were hit when advancing alone
ahead of the infantry across open ground in front of Gueudecourt. Other tanks

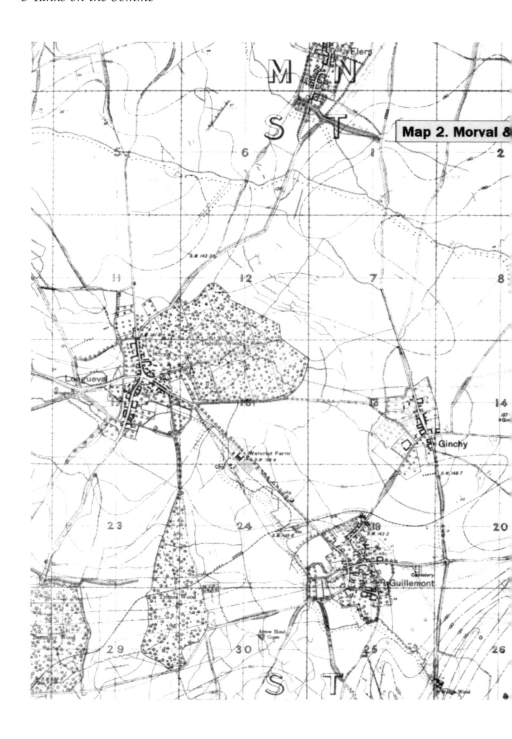

Map 2. Morval &

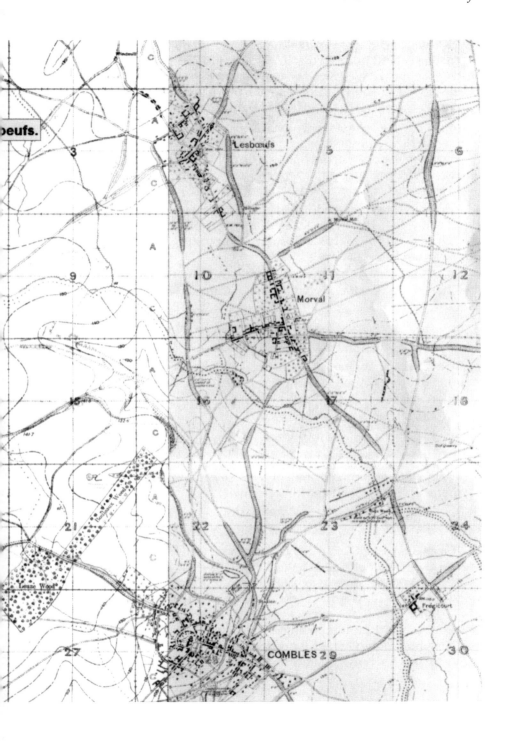

elsewhere were similarly caught without support and on exposed ground – it was, of course, hard to avoid this in places – and met a similar end.[1]

Rawlinson must have given his views on all this to Sir Douglas Haig when the latter called at Fourth Army HQ at Querrieu on the 20th. That evening, seeming to claim some of the ideas as his own, Haig wrote in his diary:

> I arranged for [*Rawlinson*] only to use tanks in the next attack where they can be hidden until the time for using them has come, and not to move them across the open in daylight for fear of them being knocked out by a direct hit by enemy guns. Under these conditions he can use them against Morval and Les Boeufs, but not against Gueudecourt.

This principle was embodied in Operational Order 59 issued earlier on this same day by the XIV Corps Commander, Lieutenant-General the Earl of Cavan. It called for the tanks in his sector to position themselves as follows, with the group letters shown:

A   To Guards Division, with position of assembly at the south-west corner of Trones Wood, under the command of Captain H.H. Hiscocks:

    722   Second Lieutenant A.L. Arnaud

    505   Second Lieutenant T.E.F. Murphy

    760   Second Lieutenant C.F.N. Ambrose

B   To 5th Division, with position of assembly likewise at the south-west corner of Trones Wood, under the command of Captain Archie Holford-Walker:

    746   Lieutenant J.P. Clarke

    741   Lieutenant J.E. Tull

    740   Lieutenant L.V. Smith

C   To 56th Division, with position of assembly at Wedge Wood, under the command of Lieutenant Sir John Dashwood:

    523   Lieutenant Sir John Dashwood

    705   Second Lieutenant A.M. Henderson/Lieutenant L.J. Bates

Later, Dashwood asked for an officer to replace Henderson, who had sprained his ankle and could not walk. Lieutenant L.J. Bates[2] was sent in his stead.

Note that no tanks were to be allotted to 6th Division – a decision perhaps connected with its unhappy experience ten days before when two of the three tanks assigned to help it destroy the Quadrilateral strong-point near Ginchy failed to appear at the time appointed. The 'lanes' left for them by the artillery meant that most of the German defenders there were left relatively unscathed, and free to inflict severe casualties on the British.

25 September

Zero on 25 September was at 12.35 p.m., but at 4.30 a.m. – eight hours earlier – the tanks of B Group moved off from Trones Wood. They proceeded round the north side of Guillemont, then took up position at T19d 5.7 in the field opposite the civil cemetery east of the village. No doubt Archie Holford-Walker had in mind Rawlinson's orders about avoiding travel in daylight but it seems odd that on arrival these three machines should have been placed in the middle of an open field, lacking the cover which Fourth Army's commander had called for, there to await the order to advance. Having travelled the 2km from their assembly point at Trones Wood at about one mile an hour, they must have arrived at around 5.45 a.m., so one hopes that the crews put the next few hours to good use by catching some sleep. Of course, the choice of location must have been determined by fear of a German bombardment of the village at Zero so for that at least the crews would have been grateful.

The orders given to them were, perhaps inevitably, left fairly vague:

After reaching the neighbourhood of our front-line troops, the further action of the tanks must depend on the tactical situation. The officers in command must necessarily act very largely on their own initiative, the main task allotted to them being to assist the infantry in every possible way by dealing with any local strong-points which may be met with and which are seen to be worrying our troops, and generally by clearing up the situation in Morval by moving down Moor Street [*the road from Ginchy*] and along Main Street [*the principal north-south street in the village*].…. The officers in charge of tanks must do their utmost, once they reach the battle area, to get in touch with the situation and find out exactly what points the infantry have reached and in what way they can best assist the operations.

Unfortunately, Clarke's 746 became ditched when only half-way between Trones Wood and Guillemont. Although the work of digging it out began quickly, the delay was serious, for it was not ready to move again until 2.45 p.m. – more than two hours after Zero. Clarke was then told simply to wait at the start point for further orders. His subsequent role on this day, if he had one, is not recorded.

Tull's 741 was also brought to an early halt, in his case by engine trouble, the platinum having come off the engine's contact breakers at 6 a.m. Repairs were completed after a delay of only an hour and a half, when Tull was told by Holford-Walker to 'proceed as far as possible without being seen by German observation balloons'. He does not seem to have proceeded very far, because as late as 10 a.m. he was still being told to get himself to the start point at Guillemont, and it was from there that he set out again at 12.55 p.m., 20 minutes after Zero. In accordance with orders he followed the line of the metre-gauge railway, approached and possibly crossed the Quadrilateral Ridge, 1,000 yards east of Ginchy, then later crashed into a trench where the tank remained stuck. It was still there at 8.30 p.m. and evidently on the following morning as well.

Smith's tank had risked the same fate as Tull's when it, too, fell into a trench – or in his case a collapsed dug-out – shortly after the start. It took four and a half hours of work to extricate it but it was freed by Zero and stood in readiness at Guillemont. Its commander later drove it along beside the railway line to the Quadrilateral, then down the road into the valley beyond. At 4.10 p.m. he took it up to the crossroads at T16a 8.6 in front of Morval, where he must have been grievously disappointed to be told on arrival that his services were no longer required, the village having already been captured by the men of 5th Division. There may, however, have been an additional reason, for a German artillery bombardment was thought to be imminent, so Captain Archie Holford-Walker simply told Smith to return to the start point near Guillemont.[3]

In contrast to B Group's early start, the War Diary tells us that A Group did not leave Trones Wood until Zero itself. This is not a simple error on the part of the diarist (probably Captain R.E. Williams, the C Company Adjutant) because the War Diary of the Guards Division specifies the same timing. With a probable speed of no more than one mile an hour over the 2.7km (1.7 miles) of shell-torn terrain, it is therefore unlikely that the tanks of A Group reached their start point immediately west of Ginchy before 2.20 p.m.

The reader may wonder what tactical plan can have called for such leisurely timing, but the fact is that the Guards Division had been told to keep its three tanks *in reserve*. There was no intention of using them, one supposes, unless some unforeseen disaster were to befall its infantry at the front. A decision to forgo their help in the early stages of fighting was no doubt in keeping with Rawlinson's instructions, but to do so throughout the battle most certainly reflects the low opinion formed of their value by the Guards Divisional Commander, Major-General G.P.T. Feilding, during the fighting of ten days before. His attitude then was justified only in part, for some of the tanks did good service, and some of their apparent shortcomings were attributable, again in part, to the Guards themselves. A different assessment of their worth was given by the Coldstream historian, who described their action on the 15th as 'a brilliant success'[4], but we have to recognise that there was at least some evidence on the 25th to support Feilding's view. Murphy's tank, for example, fell into a dug-out just after leaving Trones Wood and his crew were still digging it out at 8.30 p.m. This prompted the diarist to explain that 'these dugouts were frail and long disused. In both Smith's case and Murphy's case, there was nothing to distinguish them by.'

As for Arnaud, his tank too was brought to a halt, the problem in his case being water in the petrol. The fuel-tanks had to be emptied, then re-filled, but he still arrived at T13 Central before his scheduled time, which unfortunately the War Diary does not specify.

There is no mention of the progress made by Ambrose in tank 760, but it appears that he reached Ginchy with no major problems. He and Arnaud must then have simply settled down to sit things out and wait for further orders. Their local commander, Captain Hiscocks, was due to visit the nearby headquarters of 1st Guards Brigade at T19a 30.05 to receive any instructions from the division that there might be, but he was evidently given none. Clearly the Guards Division had concluded, rightly as it proved, that they had no need of tanks to capture Les Boeufs, but in the process their left flank suffered many casualties from the German machine guns in Point 91, which had caused the British such grievous losses on the 15th. Alas, it was only on the 26th that a tank was made available to destroy the emplacement here. Had Feilding called on Arnaud and Ambrose on the 25th many lives might have been saved. He certainly knew that Point 91 was a potent threat, for it had, as we say, given ample proof of this ten days before. The position of Point 91 is N32d 9.1, just off the top of Map 2.

One wonders what the Corps Commander, Lieutenant-General Lord Cavan, himself a former commander of the Guards Division, thought of the decision to keep its tanks idle. He had, one assumes, spent time and thought in allocating these new weapons to wherever they could be used to best effect, and although he had indeed said the tanks should be kept in reserve until needed, that need was surely established on the 25th.

During this period Dashwood and Bates in C Group, who had moved up from Wedge Wood during the night, had stood by at their start point in the small quarry (T20d 2.1) west of Leuze Wood, waiting to be called forward. They were to be deployed only in the event of the infantry attacks mounted by the three neighbouring divisions proving successful. This might at first sight seem an odd decision – perhaps even a misprint – but it was broadly in keeping with Rawlinson's instructions quoted above. They were then to help the infantry of 56th Division overcome any lingering German resistance on this right-hand flank. As soon as the order 'Tanks Advance' had been given, both machines were to proceed via the Guillemont–Combles road which separated Bouleaux and Leuze Woods and, once beyond these, to clear Stew Trench, the northern end of Loop Trench, the orchard about T22c 0.0 and the trenches in T28a on the outskirts of Combles – all of which had remained in German hands since the 15th. Ready to exploit any success achieved by the tanks, the infantry units of 167th Brigade would attack north of the road, and those of 169th Brigade to its south, while 168th Brigade would neutralise German troops in Bouleaux Wood by seizing the newly constructed trench running from the extreme north-eastern end of the wood down to the narrow-gauge railway. The tanks' final task was to block the north and north-eastern exits from Combles (about T28a 8.9 and T28b 4.7) to prevent German troops escaping from a planned pincer movement, the other arm of which took the form of a simultaneous attack mounted by the French round the eastern side of Combles.

However, the call for the services of C Group never came – not on this day at least – the infantry's capture of Morval having made their assistance unnecessary. It seems that they withdrew that same evening to their point of assembly at Wedge Wood, T26c, 0.2.

26 September

By 8.30 a.m. the next morning most of the other tanks were repositioned as follows. A Group had two of its tanks (Arnaud and Ambrose) reportedly 'east of Delville Wood' – which may be just another way of referring to their start point west of Ginchy – and one (Murphy) east of Trones Wood. B Group had two of its tanks (Clarke and Smith) at Guillemont and one (Tull) still at the Quadrilateral. Orders were later received from XIV Corps to concentrate all tanks back at Trones Wood. By 7 p.m. Hiscocks' A Group was there, but Archie Holford-Walker's B Group was still at Guillemont.

Meanwhile the two tanks of C Group were, as we say, still at Wedge Wood, or more probably the small quarry west of Leuze Wood, but at 1.40 p.m. both Dashwood and Bates were ordered forward to help 'clear up the situation south of Morval in Mutton Trench' (T17c&d and T23b), where the Germans, who had just evacuated Combles in the face of British and French attacks, had dug themselves in behind belts of wire and were holding out despite the fall of Morval itself. During the night British infantry patrols had advanced down the line of the railway into the valley between Morval and Combles and at dawn had met up with French troops emerging from the latter, but they had been unable to advance much further than the road linking the two villages. Both 12th London Regiment (56th Division, attacking from the south) and 12th Gloucestershire (5th Division, attacking from Morval) were waiting on the tanks, for it was the wish of the divisional commanders that these battalions should attempt to occupy the trench only after the tanks had subdued it.

Unfortunately both machines were put out of action, so the infantry operation was cancelled. Dashwood, in the female tank 523, had 'bellied' on a tree-stump at the corner of the sunken road T17a 65.60, so it is clear that he had passed through Morval in order to attack Mutton Trench from the north, originally its rear. Bates, in the male 705, had become ditched in square T16c, which would seem to indicate that he had been planning to attack Mutton Trench from its front, the south-west, because from T16c it was a comparatively short distance to Sinew Trench, and thence over the Morval–Combles road to the target.

Gunner W. Dawson, a member of Dashwood's crew, later recalled that having waited

> in the shelter of a small hillside stone quarry for two or three days another officer, Lieutenant Sir John Dashwood, who had been in a Highland regiment, [*was*] appointed to our tank, when we, along with another of our section tanks (No. 4 section), went forward to attack Morval. This went well until, on the right of Morval, we became stuck on the stump of a tree in a sunken road. The belly of the machine was jammed fast on the stump with the tracks just going round ineffectively.[5]

27 September

In the early hours of 27 September Dashwood sent a message asking for petrol and oil to be sent out to him. Evidently he, and perhaps Bates too, had used up much of their fuel in the advance and in the effort to extricate themselves. Supplies were duly sent to them by pack transport at 3 a.m., but Dashwood now realised that, being so near the still unsubdued Mutton Trench, there was no prospect of an early recovery of his own machine. He therefore returned with his crew, on foot, all the way back to the Loop T 27b, where he reported to his headquarters. Totally exhausted, they were given time to rest before walking back to Morval again. All of them, including the Premier Baronet of Great Britain[6] – 'quite a splendid fellow' according to his crew – were laden down with picks and shovels with which they finally managed to release tank 523. It arrived back at the Loop on 1 October.

At 2.10 a.m. on the 27th orders were received from XIV Corps for the three tanks from Trones Wood – those of Arnaud, Ambrose and the now-recovered Murphy, none of which were needed by the Guards now safely established in Les Boeufs – to go forward again in another attempt to help 'clear up the situation in Mutton Trench'. They moved out at 3 a.m. and arrived at the Quadrilateral Ridge at 9.30 a.m. However, fearful that they might not arrive on time, Holford-Walker had decided to send two additional tanks – those of Clarke and Smith – from the nearer base at Guillemont, these arriving at the ridge by 8.30 a.m. He then spent several hours in urgent talks with infantry commanders in various locations, including 168th Brigade of 56th Division, who were to take part in the operation. While he was there the brigadier told him that Dashwood had been ordered – we do not know by whom – to resume his attack as soon as he had dug out his tank. Holford-Walker realised that, without further planning and coordination, such a move promised chaos. He therefore agreed a plan of action with the brigadier of 60th Brigade (part of the 20th Division, due to relieve the 5th later in the day) but a sudden bombardment of Clarke's and Smith's positions near the ridge showed that the Germans had spotted these tanks at least, and had found their range. Holford-Walker decided to call both tanks back into reserve at Guillemont.

The incident seems to have persuaded XIV Corps that the use of tanks in this area was too risky an enterprise, for the Germans now knew, if they did not know before, that Morval was about to be attacked by Britain's new armoured fighting vehicles – the *panzerkampfwagen* or *panzerkraftwagen*. The War Diary, which gives a somewhat confusing account of these events (as does Dawson), seems to imply that the three A Group tanks, though nearer to Morval, remained hidden from German view. They certainly did not move during daylight on the 27th and were only withdrawn to Trones Wood in the course of the following night.

28 September

So by the 28th all the tanks, including those of Dashwood and Bates, had left the area. The task of finally capturing Mutton Trench was then left to 20th Division, which had relieved the 5th, and to the French 2nd Division, which had relieved the 56th.

Field Guide

IGN Maps 2408E & 2508O

Trones Wood (Bois des Troncs to the French) lies just north of the D64 road linking Montauban with Guillemont. In accordance with orders, the tanks in B Group would have driven from there around the southern end of the wood, then across the fields north of the D64 rather than staying on it, in order to reach their start point north-east of Guillemont, in the field opposite the civil cemetery.

The tanks of A Group would have continued on, some distance to the left of B Group, in order to reach their own start point at the corner of the field immediately west of Ginchy, just beyond a poplar-fringed cattle pasture, which is also where the tanks operating with the 3rd Coldstream Guards had assembled on the 15th. To see this, drive out of Guillemont on the road (known as 'Green Street' to the British) signposted to Ginchy. In the village, turn first left along the road signposted to Longueval. Immediately after passing the pasture, T13 Central is next to you in the field on your right.

Now turn round and re-enter Ginchy. At the main crossroads in the village turn right, into the Chemin du Roy. At 600m there is a hump in the road which shows where the light railway crossed on its way to the Quadrilateral, by the trees over your left shoulder. Its course through the Vallée Boulan – so shallow as to be almost invisible – is still marked on the 1996 IGN map. After another 300m you arrive at a crossroads, marked on one corner by a memorial to men of 20th Division who fought in this same area. Go straight over and down the hill to Wedge Wood, named after its shape. It was here that Dashwood and Bates in C Group made a preliminary halt and awaited orders to proceed to their start point. Before you leave, look just east of the wood at the embankments, now shrouded in bushes, where numerous dug-outs housed battalion and brigade headquarters throughout the latter part of the Somme campaign.

Now retrace your path as if going back up to the crossroads, but after 200m or so you will see a branch road turning off to the right. Follow this round and you pass beside the 'quarry', now hidden beneath a stretch of vegetation, more extensive than the trench map leads you to expect. Here was the start point of Dashwood and Bates where they waited for the summons to battle.

Drive up onto the Guillemont–Combles road and turn right, heading for the two woods in front of you – Leuze Wood ('Lousy Wood') on the right and Bouleaux Wood ('Bully Wood') on the left. Had they been called forward, Dashwood and Bates would have driven between the two in order to help clear the trenches beyond. These were Stew Trench, more or less parallel to the road in the field to your left, and Loop Trench, which joined the road at right-angles from the field on your right, about 50m short of the water-tower.

But the call did not come, or at least not in the form earlier envisaged. Instead, the two tanks were required to help attack Morval the following day, the 26th, and to do this they could have taken one of several routes – via the Quadrilateral and the road running down beside the railway, or down the track which leads from Leuze Wood past the post-war memorial to Cedric Charles Dickens[7], or alongside the north-western face of Bouleaux Wood. We are inclined to believe that it was the first of these, if only because it afforded slightly more cover from view.

The Quadrilateral, now in British hands, was certainly on the route allotted to Tull and Smith in B Group, coming from Guillemont on the 25th. Indeed Tull is said to have reached somewhere near the 'ridge' here before crashing into a trench. The ridge is a fairly gentle feature, but one which on the 15th had blocked the British view of German positions further back. Nearer the Ginchy–Morval road the dip is more pronounced.

The strong-point itself, surrounding spot height 153, was captured on the 18th without the aid of tanks. It lay 900m east of Ginchy, immediately right of the road before it drops down on its way to Morval. Today just a patch of beaten earth and chalk, its northern portion can be seen in the triangle formed by the road and the former light railway (Le Tortillard), but it extended well into the field to the south. It proved a most formidable obstacle, accounting for hundreds of British casualties on the 15th. It was down this same road that Smith travelled on the 25th, Dashwood and Bates on the 26th, and the three tanks of A Group on the 27th. Trees and shrubs now mask the course of the

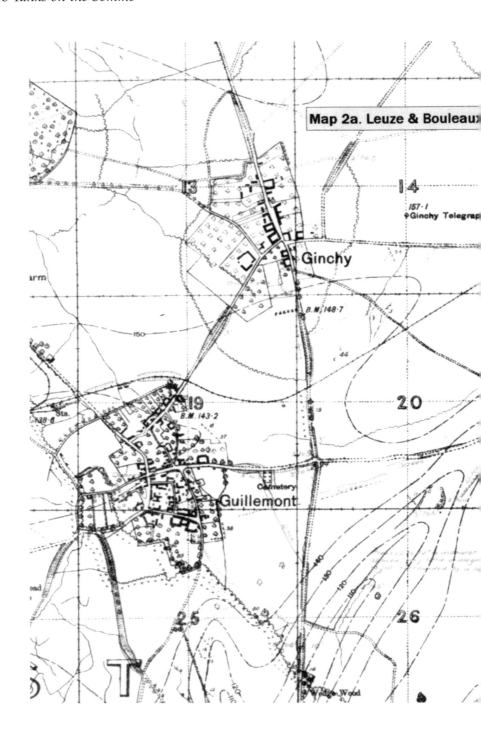

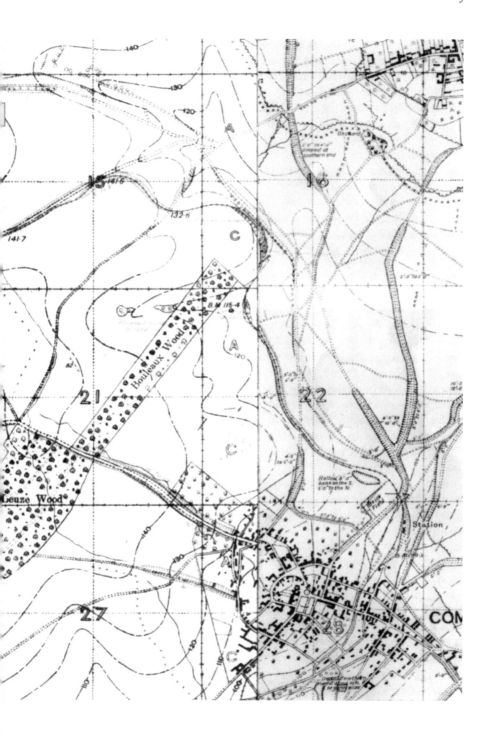

railway which ran down the slope beside them.

Reaching the valley below (Vallée du Marécage) Dashwood began his climb up to the village but he was then stopped, and ordered back, at the sunken crossroads at T16a 8.6. This no longer has the shape that it had, the northern branch having been filled in, but a small chapel on the bank of what is now a T-junction can be seen from some distance away. When the British troops arrived here they built a strong-point to defend their gains, basing it on an earlier German strong-point which, positioned on top of the south-west quadrant of the crossroads, caused many casualties among the British advancing down from Bouleaux Wood and the Quadrilateral.

A few metres further down the side road here was where Mince Trench crossed it, this being taken by the British early on, once the strong-point at the crossroads had been captured. But to see the area of Mutton Trench, carry on up the main road to Morval and take the D11E exit signposted to Combles, but only for 200m. Do not follow the bend to the right but – with very great care, for this is a blind corner – keep straight ahead, onto a rough track and park your car. You are now on the exact spot where Dashwood's tank became stuck on the tree stump. In 1916 this track led eventually, via the tiny village of Frégicourt (in the French sector, destroyed in the fighting), across to the main Bapaume–Péronne highway, but nowadays it is blocked, first by the TGV high-speed railway, then by the massive structure where the A1 and A2 motorways merge. Just visible are the few trees remaining to mark what to the British was Haie Wood (Bois de la Haie), now half-buried under many tons of concrete. Much nearer to you, on the right of the track, at a distance varying from 50m to 150m, lay Mutton Trench, which you are now seeing from the German side. From its position just east of the crest it gave a superb view over the French attacking forces to the south and, certainly from any forward observation posts that it may have had, over the British positions as well. An even better view of these latter was obtainable from the adjacent Meat Trench and Mince Trench but these, together with part of Mutton Trench itself, were taken by the British during the first afternoon's fighting. Until then the German occupants overlooked Vallée Vircholle and Vallée du Marecage and would easily have seen British troops on the north-facing slopes of the Quadrilateral Ridge known as La Marcaille and Terres Vieilles.

Whereas Dashwood lay immobilised near the southern exit from Morval, Bates was said to be stuck at a point in Square T16c. We do not know where exactly this was but clearly it was somewhere near the railway embankment, where a German emplacement of no fewer than four machine guns and five *minenwerfer* had been captured the day before. These were at T16c 45.70, no doubt hidden in the trees which still line the route of the now-vanished railway, and well sited to confront any British troops advancing towards them along the north-west face of Bouleaux Wood. The men of 56th Division had later pressed on further along the railway and by dawn on the 26th had met up with French troops coming round from the east side of Combles and through its centre, following the fleeing Germans. The War Diary of 56th Division says that Bates 'returned without attempting to reach the objective Mutton Trench' but we think that the implied criticism here is unfair. Bates had almost certainly turned off the main Ginchy–Morval road in order to advance along the valley to attack Mutton Trench from the south-west or south, while Dashwood came down from the north. It is just unfortunate that both tanks became ditched in the process.

---

[1]   In this one area, D5 (Blowers) and D6 (Legge) were destroyed on the 15th; D9 (Huffam), D14 (Court) and D11 (Pearsall) were all destroyed on the 16th.

[2]   Lieutenant (later Captain) Leonard John Bates died, aged 34, on 10 November 1917 and is buried in Grangegorman Military Cemetery in Ireland, Grave CE Officers 8.

[3]   The War Diaries tell us that an observer of the RFC reported having seen two tanks at near-dusk on the 25th in square T9 Central. One of them, he said, was shooting. We cannot identify this machine and we are not aware of any tank being in the area at the time. One explanation could be that the airman gave the wrong time and the wrong map reference, and meant T15 Central, the square below T9, which is indeed on the way to Morval. The tank could thus have been that of Victor Smith, with Tull following somewhere behind. But neither of them would have been shooting, we believe, and the report would thus appear to have been garbled.

[4]   Sir J.F.G. Ross of Bladenburg, *The Coldstream Guards 1914-1918*.

[5]   The reference to sections is confusing as there had been a degree of reorganisation during and after 15 September. Dashwood was originally in No. 3 Section, and Bates in No. 2. The officer in No. 4 Section was Henderson, whom Bates had replaced.

[6]   *Premier* Baronet of Great Britain, because the Dashwood baronetcy was the first to be created after the Act of Union in 1707. Any baronetcy created before then was an English baronetcy.

[7]   The monument is to the memory of Major Cedric Charles Dickens, nephew of the novelist, killed near here on 9 September 1916.

Chapter 3

Gueudecourt: 25–26 September[1]

One of the tasks given to the men of Fourth Army on 15 September was the capture of Gueudecourt by 14th Division, but although it lay less than 1.6km north-east of the newly won British positions at Flers, the village remained beyond their grasp. Despite tank support, the infantry casualties were too heavy and in consequence the advance gradually faded away, the tanks eventually finding themselves unprotected and isolated in enemy-held territory. One of these, Second Lieutenant A.H. Blowers' D5 (*Dolphin*), penetrated as far as the formidable Gird Line, which barred the southern approach to the village, before it had to turn back, only to be destroyed by a German battery closer to Flers. Another tank, Second Lieutenant R.C. Legge's D6, had approached Gueudecourt from the south-west but it too was destroyed when only 90m from the German defences. Further attempts were made the following day, 16 September, by Second Lieutenant V. Huffam in D9 (*Dolly*), Second Lieutenant G.F. Court in D14, and Second Lieutenant H.G. Pearsall in D11 (*Die Hard*), but all three were knocked out by German artillery fire.

Some progress – slow, costly and limited – was achieved by the infantry in the days following these attacks, but GHQ pressed for further efforts to be made as soon as practicable. Bad weather hampered large-scale operations for a while but orders were issued for a major attack to be launched on the 25th, in conjunction with the assault further to the right against Morval and Les Boeufs, the tanks' part in which has already been described. At Gueudecourt the infantry's part immediately south of the village was to be played by 64th and 110th Brigades of 21st Division, positioned either side of the track known as Watling Street. Further left, south-west of the village, was 165th Brigade of 55th Division.

As well as facing the double trench of the Gird Line south of Gueudecourt,

Map 3. Gueudecourt.

the British had to contend with the particularly deadly machine-gun emplacement on the eastern flank, shown on the maps as Point 91, N32d 9.1. This had poured murderous fire on all the attackers within its range ever since the battle opened on 15 September. Positioned at the junction of Gas Alley (not shown on map 3 but which ran in an almost straight line from Point 91 to T1d 0.3 south-east of Flers) and Gird Trench, it had dominated the left of the Guards Division and the right of 14th Division, causing hundreds of casualties. Several infantry and artillery attacks had been mounted in an effort to destroy it, all to no avail. So great was the concern about the threat which it posed to the British advance that General Sir Henry Rawlinson himself – commander of an army numbering many thousands of men – spent time at a conference discussing what should be done about this one machine-gun post!

It appears that four tanks were originally earmarked for an attempt on the 25th to destroy the guns at Point 91 and those elsewhere threatening the British south of Gueudecourt. According to the personal diary kept by D Company's adjutant, Captain A.G. Woods, the tank commanders included the following, all of whom had come to grief on the 15th: Captain S.S. Sellick (whose tank 753, D19, had ditched before going into action that day), Second Lieutenant H.G. Head (728, D3, ditched alongside the Longueval–Flers road but recovered on the 18th) and Captain G. Nixon (719, D12, set on fire by a shell on the west side of Flers). The fourth officer was Second Lieutenant Charles Storey, who, on his way to support 14th Division on the 15th, had been badly ditched near Delville Wood and had taken no part in the day's events.[2]

On 25 September Zero hour all along the line was 12.35 p.m. When the whistles blew, the men of 64th Brigade stepped bravely out from their makeshift trenches east of Flers, with 10th King's Own Yorkshire Light Infantry on the right and 1st East Yorkshire on the left. To their left again were 9th and 8th Leicester Regiments of 110th Brigade. And as they moved to the attack, all four battalions were immediately brought under the most intense machine-gun fire.

Their losses were appalling. 10th KOYLI suffered most, being closest to the guns at Point 91, but 1st East Yorkshires also lost, as did the Leicesters further left, their line of advance caught in terrible enfilade from Point 91 and Gas Alley.

It was, as we say, in the hope of avoiding losses such as these that XV Corps had arranged for the tanks' support. However, it appears that, of the four, Sellick had dropped out, apparently because he had been injured, and Nixon's tank had been disabled by a shell. Head's had broken a track in Flers on its way forward and could not be repaired in time; it was subsequently re-allocated, possibly to support a later advance planned by the New Zealand Division.

That left Storey in D4. He was on hand and ready to press ahead but Major-General Campbell, the commander of 21st Division, concluded that, with just one tank in support, any attempt by his division on the 25th was doomed to failure, the men being much reduced in numbers and physically exhausted. He asked for a postponement, but this was initially refused by his Corps Commander, Lieutenant-General H.S. Horne. Campbell then persisted in his plea and eventually the attack was put off to the following day.

Early on the 26th therefore, Storey's 'new' D4 – a replacement for his earlier machine but bearing the same designation – moved out of Flers along Good Street and took up position on Gird Trench.[3] It had been delayed by the poor state of the ground but it now turned right at a trench block erected the previous evening by 8th Leicesters at N26c 4.5 and began its slow progress along the German-held portion of the trench. Closely followed by a bombing party of 7th Leicesters, supported further back by C and D Companies of that battalion carrying a supply of a thousand grenades, Storey enfiladed the trench with deadly effect. The occupants began to move swiftly away down the trench towards the south, gathering in numbers as they went. Some chose to seek shelter in the dug-outs but were ordered to come out, the alternative being grenades tossed in by the Leicesters lining the parapet and parados. Many others scrambled up ladders and tried to make a run for it but were immediately shot down. Others were killed by bullets from an RFC aircraft flying low overhead. Meanwhile the flood of men now jamming the trench moved ahead as fast as their comrades further on would allow. They were forced on, pursued by the monstrous apparition breathing death and fiery terror from its front and sides. The spectacle was extraordinary.

There was a temporary check at Watling Street, where the tank plunged down the bank onto the road below, but Storey then carried on for another 180m before turning off to the left, reportedly heading for the Causeway, a track leading into Gueudecourt from the neighbouring village of Les Boeufs. Storey's tank was said to have been spotted here, at N33a 0.8, by an aircraft of the RFC at noon, so he may have paused here before continuing his advance, perhaps in order to attend to his wounds and those of his crew. However, we think it unlikely that he would have chosen this particular approach, given the need to press on, for it would have involved going round two sides of a triangle to get to the entrance of Gueudecourt at the Shrine (so called because a statue of the Virgin stands nearby).

In switching his attack on to Gueudecourt, Storey must have thought that the operation against Gird Trench was going smoothly enough – which it certainly was, for the bombers carried on with no check at all. Some of the defenders surrendered to the Leicesters on the spot but most of them simply moved up the trench in a long stream until they emerged, ironically, at Point

91, near which the Guards Division was waiting to escort them back to the prisoner-of-war cages.

Storey, whose first tank had ditched in Delville Wood on 15 September and who had taken no further part in the battle that day, had now proved in spectacular fashion that the new weapon of war could bring success to those who used it well. He and his crew had been instrumental in capturing eight officers and 362 men and in killing many others now left in the trench or in the fields around it. The Leicester casualties were two killed and two wounded. This was surely a just revenge for the slaughter of the British below Point 91. The *Official History* notes that, according to German accounts, Storey's tank annihilated the I/6th Bavarian Regiment in front of Gueudecourt.

What now happened to Storey is unclear. The D Company War Diary says simply that he returned because he had run out of petrol. He may have done so, but not yet. Otherwise why would he have headed away from his base and towards the enemy still in Gueudecourt? Almost certainly he thought he still had work to do, as indeed one eye-witness testified. Major C.A. Milward, second-in-command of 10th KOYLI, who had watched Storey's progress down Gird Trench with evident wonder and admiration, met him later on and said:

> We heard from the tank man who had returned, covered with blood and bound up, that he had crawled his tank over the village and, instead of meeting fifty Germans as expected, he had come across five hundred whom he had taken on. In the end he had run out of petrol but had managed to get back himself.

We do not know Storey's route through Gueudecourt but to have engaged 500 of the enemy there, with few if any infantry to lend him support, is surely a measure of his courage, but his other exploits on this day had already earned him a place in the ranks of heroes, for he had saved dozens if not hundreds of British lives. He had, however, paid a price, he himself being badly wounded in the eye and four of his crew being wounded by 'splash' – molten lead from bullets hitting crevices in the armour – and by the hot splinters of steel flaking off the interior of the tank whenever it was hit by machine-gun fire on the outside. Given the circumstances, Storey was right to head home but, on its way back through the British lines, his tank became 'slightly ditched', according to the records. It was abandoned and Storey and his crew of seven returned to Flers. A party of men went out later to recover the tank but as they were trying to move it the tracks broke.

The collapse of their defences in the Gird Line evidently convinced the Germans that the village itself was no longer tenable. They withdrew northwards, their positions in Gueudecourt being taken before noon by British infantry patrols gradually filtering in from 64th Brigade. Later, cavalry patrols from the South Irish Horse and 19th Indian Lancers were sent round the east side of the village but were heavily shelled when they neared the far side. Other cavalry units, dismounted, entered the village, as did elements of 110th Brigade, who dug in on the north side as the cavalry withdrew.

Storey's part in the capture of Gueudecourt was recognised by Sir Douglas Haig, who wrote in his diary for the day:

> A strong redoubt which was holding out between Les Boeufs and Gueudecourt was captured early this morning. A tank was sent against it and many aeroplanes flew over at about 500 feet elevation. The enemy at once held up his hands. Two officers and 120 men surrendered [*sic, actually many more*].

Haig had, of course, warned Rawlinson not to expose his tanks in front of Gueudecourt, where they would be vulnerable to enemy artillery fire, but doubtless Rawlinson decided that the proximity of the tank to the enemy's own troops justified the risk.

In the event, he was right. And Haig would have been right, too, had he later quoted this success to rebut the arguments of those – including Swinton – who had argued against using the tanks in 'driblets'. Storey's achievement must have been precisely what the Commander-in-Chief had hoped to gain when he decided that, once their existence was known to the enemy, he had little to lose by using the tanks wherever and whenever he could, in whatever numbers were available, in order to help push the enemy back. His warning to Rawlinson notwithstanding, he must have been delighted at the outcome.

Storey was later awarded the DSO, the citation reading:

> For gallantry and initiative in command of tank D14 [*sic*] on 26th September, when he was called upon by GOC 110th Brigade to clear up certain trenches south-east of Gueudecourt which were holding up the infantry. Lieutenant Storey took his car up and down each trench, working until all his petrol was exhausted and only two of the crew were unwounded. He is reported as having been responsible for the taking of between 200 and 300 prisoners. I consider this to be the best tank performance up to date.

The identification of Storey's tank as D14 is incorrect, for this was the company number of Second Lieutenant G.F. Court's machine, destroyed during an earlier attack on Gueudecourt on 16 September. Ten days later Storey's D4 – his 'new' D4, apparently a male tank armed with 57mm cannon – was left at the side of the road leading north out of Flers.

Field Guide
IGN Map 2407E
The south-western end of Good Street near Flers has now been ploughed under, so to see where Storey's tank began its historic journey, go first into

Gueudecourt. Drive up past the right-hand side of what used to be the church (rebuilt in the 1920s, demolished in 1996, replaced by a small belfry in 1998) and go towards the gates at the top. Do not enter them but turn right, then left, eventually coming out into the fields. Walk down the track (this is the north-eastern end of Good Street) for 320m and you are standing on Gird Trench at the spot where Court's tank D14 was destroyed on the 16th. At a distance of 130m on your left (roughly south-south-east) lay D4's start point on the 26th at N26c 4.5. The farm-tracks in its immediate vicinity have long disappeared so, depending on the season and on the crops, you may or may not be able to follow the course of Gird Trench at this point. Note, however, that it bears roughly south-eastwards before crossing Pilgrims Way, then Watling Street (Chemin des Guilmonniers) where there is a considerable drop, which must have given a bit of a jolt to the commander and crew of D4. Nothing daunted, they continued for a short distance up the further stretch of Gird Trench, which ran more or less parallel to the new, post-war road branching up from a small pond on Watling Street. The trench converged on this road at a corner 700m beyond the pond. Here stood Point 91, its dominating position being immediately apparent. Now turn back (with care, as the road is narrow) towards Gueudecourt. After leaving the Leicesters to carry on the work of clearing the trench, Storey must then have made for the Shrine crossroads. We cannot follow his route through Gueudecourt but we have a photograph of a tank, wrecked on the road leading north out of Flers, next to D11. This was Pearsall's *Die Hard*, which was knocked out on the 16th.

---

[1]   Parts of this chapter have appeared already in the author's earlier book, *Flers and Gueudecourt*.

[2]   Other papers suggest that, apart from Head and Nixon, the four included Lieutenant Stuart Hastie (whose D17, *Dinnaken*, was the first to enter Flers on the 15th 'with the British army cheering behind' but which was now left disabled on the battlefield, there serving as a joint headquarters for the commanders of 64th and 110th Brigades), and Second Lieutenant Victor Huffam (whose D9, *Dolly*, was knocked out on the 16th). But this list is suspect, if only because it does not include Storey, who we know was indeed involved on the 26th.

[3]   It is possible that Storey made his approach up Pilgrims Way but we think this unlikely.

Chapter 4

Martinpuich: 25 September

Compared with the operations of Fourth Army elsewhere on this day, the part played by III Corps may seem rather limited in scope, consisting of apparently minor operations by its 1st, 50th and 23rd Divisions. Only two tanks were to be involved.

However, the possibility of an earlier operation, with somewhat greater tank participation, had been discussed at a III Corps conference on 20 September, the intention being to employ four machines – two with 1st Division and two with 50th Division – to support an infantry advance northwards towards Le Sars from the ground between Martinpuich and two former German redoubts known as the Cough Drop and the Starfish situated further to the east. This plan was almost immediately abandoned, however, mainly because of the need to coordinate any operations in this area with those due to take place elsewhere, for on this same day Sir Douglas Haig directed General Rawlinson to hand over to the Reserve Army as many tanks as Fourth Army could spare, to enable General Gough to mount an attack on Thiepval, perhaps as early as the 23rd if the weather allowed. Of the twenty which he held, Rawlinson decided he needed to retain twelve, thus releasing eight for Gough's operation.

In the event, III Corps revised its plans entirely. Now, on 25 September, it was only 23rd Division, on the left of the Corps, that was to have tank assistance. Two machines were assigned to support an attack on the Germans' front line, now established, following their reverses on the 15th, not only in the further part of Mill Road, which ran north and north-west of Martinpuich, but more especially in the trench known as Twenty-Sixth Avenue. This was a long trench – originally a communication trench – stretching all the way from the Flers Line south of Le Sars over to Courcelette, this latter having now been captured by the Canadians. Its name derived from the fact that, nearer the

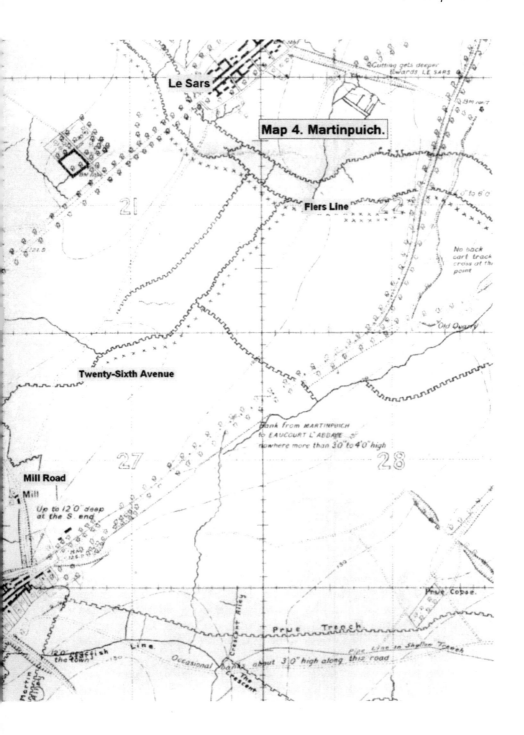

Le Sars

Cutting gets deeper towards LE SARS

8m row 7

Map 4. Martinpuich.

Flers Line

4'0" to 6'0"

No back cart track cross at this point

Old Quarry

Twenty-Sixth Avenue

Bank from MARTINPUICH to EAUCOURT L'ABBAYE nowhere more than 3'0" to 4'0" high

Mill Road

Mill

Up to 12'0" deep at the S. end

Prue Copse.

Prue Trench

120" deep ffisth the town Line

Occasional banks about 3'0" high along this road

Pipe Line in Skyline Trench

Crescent Alley

The Crescent

Martin

village, it traversed square M26 on the map. To the Germans it was Bayern Graben.[1]

The infantry assault was to be mounted by 10th Northumberland Fusiliers of 68th Brigade. As in other sectors on this day, Zero was 12.35 p.m.

For reasons unstated, III Corps announced at 11 a.m. on the 24th that tanks would *not* be used in the attack the following day. It so happened that one of the machines allocated to the operation had ditched on its way up to the start point, but this was not known at Corps level until mid-afternoon, so cannot have been the reason behind the change of plan. The news had been announced by 'O.C. Tanks' (possibly Major Frank Summers but more probably a local tank commander), who told Corps staff that the machine would be out of action for two days.[2]

Despite this, the staff at III Corps changed their minds yet again, and announced at 7.10 p.m. that both tanks would, after all, be used. The grounds for this second reversal of policy remain obscure, because the tank under repair was at the time still out of action. In the event, it was repaired by 9.15 a.m. the following morning and could have taken part in the operation, but by then the presence of fourteen German observation balloons floating in the sky not far away made it inadvisable to move the tank up to the assembly point in daylight. III Corps asked if the RFC could send up an aircraft to chase the balloons away but the record does not say what the response was. Sadly, the report submitted just after Zero from an artillery Forward Observation Officer (FOO) to the effect that both tanks were going well was quite untrue.

The tank which did go into action on the 25th was D18, a male, no. 743. It had been commanded on 15 September by Second Lieutenant L.C. Bond, who had taken it up as far as the north-western edge of Flers, but had been wounded in the course of the fighting there. The tank's new commander was Lieutenant A.J. Enoch, whose own machine D7 had ditched on the 15th at an early stage in the advance northwards from Longueval.

At 2.45 a.m. ten days later Enoch in D18 reached the assembly point at the bottom of Gun Pit Road (Gunpit Trench on Map 4), which wound its way north-westwards from Martinpuich, up through a deep cutting towards the crossroads later known as Le Ballon. His companion, now missing, would have continued up this road because he had been given the extreme western end of Twenty-Sixth Avenue as his target, from Point 29 (M26c 2.9), which lay 250m north-east of the crossroads, across to M26 Central. Enoch had been given the eastern end, from M26 Central along to Point 53 (M26b 5.3), where Twenty-Sixth Avenue formed a junction with the trench leading up from the village. The name of this latter is not certain but was probably Park Alley.

However, the non-appearance of the second tank persuaded the commander of 68th Brigade, Brigadier-General G.N. Colville, to cancel the Northumberlands' attack on the western end of the German line. Effort was now to be concentrated against the eastern end – the portion already assigned to Enoch, but now working from right to left of the target, from Point 53 over to M26 Central. After dealing with any opposition there he was to proceed to Point 29 then move off, through the Canadian lines, and back down the main road to the south-west. Gun Pit Road, the route assigned earlier to his companion, would not of course have provided Enoch with the best access to Point 53 over to the east, nor indeed would the route leading due north across country from M26d 0.3 near Martinpuich that had been assigned to him under the original plan. At short notice, 68th Brigade therefore asked him to carry out a reconnaissance to determine a better, more easterly route. This he did at 6 p.m. on the 24th and it was this route that he followed the next morning. In this the brigade staff showed foresight, for at the time of the reconnaissance it was thought that no tanks would be used.

Alas, Enoch's appearance on the battlefield prompted the Germans to unleash a torrent of shells on the Poor Bloody Infantry even before they had left their trenches. And shortly after beginning their attack the Northumberlands sustained further heavy losses from machine-gun and rifle fire from Twenty-Sixth Avenue. The survivors struggled forward but soon faltered, then went to ground. Attempts were made to re-start the advance and small isolated parties approached to within 55m of the target but were there struck down. The Northumberlands' account says that Enoch, moving alongside Park Alley, trundled up towards Point 53 then swung left, as his orders had said he should. A report by a contact patrol of the RFC confirms that he was later seen advancing towards M26b 3.2.

However, it would appear that, seeing the infantry in disarray, Enoch soon concluded that the whole enterprise was now doomed, so he 'then backed down across Push Alley, out of action'. Whether this means he reversed his machine at this point is not clear, but we think this unlikely.

RFC observers placed the point of D18's demise at M26d 6.6, which was just in front of Park Alley, whereas the War Diary of D Company says it was further on, at M26d 8.8, which would be consistent with the reference to Enoch 'crossing' a trench before coming to rest. In neither case, however, can the trench have been Push Alley, since this ran much closer to the village before extending towards the Mill.

If the above is an accurate account of Enoch's progress it would explain why RFC reports later claimed that he had described a complete circle before coming to rest in territory held by the British, just south of their trench-block. Being ditched, the tank provided a sitting target for German artillery, apparently guided by their observation balloons gathered in the sky to the north-east. Three members of the crew were wounded by flakes of steel struck off the interior surface of the tank, and by 'splash' from bullets entering the crevices and loop-holes. They later abandoned the tank.

Several months later Captain Shirley-Jones of D Company, 8th Worcestershires, sketched the wreck during the time that his unit was lying in support of the rest of the battalion further forward near Le Sars.

It may be thought that this action at Martinpuich on 25 September represented a graphic example of the futility of using the tanks in 'driblets', which is what their main proponent, Ernest Swinton, had warned against in February 1916 while the machine was still on the drawing-board. And even if the second tank had been available the result might well have been the same.

But *was* the operation futile? In the knowledge that the following day would see a major Reserve Army attack launched along a front from Courcelette to Thiepval, Haig must surely have concluded that a necessary preliminary was an effort to clear its flank of all German forces there – including those in Twenty-Sixth Avenue – that were capable of threatening the Canadians' advance. That was what Enoch was attempting to do. Consider the achievement of the following day, described in our previous chapter. In that operation, originally designed to take place at the same time as Enoch's, another single tank, commanded by Second Lieutenant Charles Storey, had been instrumental in annihilating an enemy force of several hundred in Gird Trench and Point 91 and thus opening the way to the capture of Gueudecourt. That might have happened here at Martinpuich, too.

Field Guide

IGN Map 2407E

At the north-east end of Martinpuich there are three exits; one on the left leads up to the main Albert–Bapaume road; one leads straight ahead to Eaucourt l'Abbaye and Le Barque; the third, a narrow lane on the right, leads past a small chapel or oratoire up into the fields lying east of the village. We shall be visiting the first two roads again later on, but for the moment take a few minutes to explore the lane on the right. It was from this end of the village that the roughly parallel Starfish Line and Prue Trench extended east to the former German redoubts Starfish and Cough Drop, respectively 2250m and 1800m away, which we shall also be visiting in a later chapter. The British held only the extremities of these trenches, the middle parts of which together formed the First Objective for the infantry in the attack planned at the III Corps conference on 20 September. The tanks were evidently to be used to envelop the German defenders in a form of pincer movement, the left-hand arm of which would be the two tanks of 50th Division, using the road that you are now on. At the start, this road diverges increasingly from Prue Trench which lay, on average, 200–300m to your right, with the Starfish Line beyond it still nearer to the British. After a right-hand bend the road proceeds in a straight line and begins to close on Prue Trench once more, eventually passing two adjacent copses on the left. The nearer of these (it is difficult to distinguish between them) was Prue Copse to the British, but Bois Carré on the IGN map. The further one dates from after the war but is shown on the latest IGN editions as sharing the name of its neighbour. The road from this point begins to deteriorate but the Cough Drop lay to the east just over the ridge, immediately south-east of where the IGN map now shows two tracks crossing at spot height 133m near the area known as Les Fiefs. The Starfish was 450m further to its south, in the south-west corner of the junction at spot height 129m near Les Dix-Neuf. After an initial swing southwards, two tanks from 1st Division were due to advance alongside Prue Copse and join up with the pair from Martinpuich at the Seven Elms crossroads at M28d 5.4.

As we say, this original plan was abandoned on the 20th, soon after it was formulated, as being less relevant to GHQ's requirement for tank support elsewhere. The new plan called for two tanks to assemble at the lowest point of Gun Pit Road (Rue de Courcelette), which leads north from near the south-western end of Martinpuich, but Enoch arrived there alone. From here he was to enter the field on his right but the bank leading up to it at this point is steep, so he may have preferred to enter it over the gentler slopes further east along Rue Basse. He then set out from his start point on the British front line, M26d 0.3.

To see the rest of his route, go back to the north-eastern end of the village and take the left-hand exit, Mill Road. After about 300m the Mill, of which nothing now remains except a few half-buried bricks which once formed its base, stood on the summit at the edge of the field on your left. (This was 60–70m short of the track you see ahead of you on the right, which no longer follows the route shown on the trench map.) Some 130m or so further into the field beyond the Mill is M26d 8.8. Proceed another 300m along the road and you are on the German front line in Twenty-Sixth Avenue.

---

[1]   The words Avenue, Lane and Alley were usually, but by no means always, reserved for trenches leading up to the front line from the rear. These were *communication* trenches. Sometimes the terms were applied also to trenches linking several adjacent communication trenches in the rear. *Fighting* trenches were those which ran along the front line and its immediate rear and were more often called simply Trench, the word Line being reserved more for a major trench work or system of trenches. In the case of Twenty Sixth Avenue, its original siting as a communication trench when the German front line lay further west later made it admirably suited as a fighting trench to counter the new British threat from Martinpuich in the south, although not from the Canadian threat now posed from Courcelette.

[2]   In his report on the action submitted on 30 September the commander of III Corps, Lieutenant-General Sir William Pulteney, said the missing tank had been due to approach up the Albert–Bapaume road but this was not so. He was confusing it with a tank operating with the Canadians the next day. See our later chapter on the fighting around Courcelette.

Chapter 5

Eaucourt l'Abbaye:
1 October

Following the capture by Fourth Army of Combles, Morval, Les Boeufs and Gueudecourt during the fighting on 25–26 September, and of Thiepval by the Reserve Army (see later chapter), General Rawlinson set out his further intentions in an Operation Order on 28 September. His immediate concern was to straighten the line in front of III Corps by capturing the farm buildings at Eaucourt l'Abbaye – sited on the remains of an old monastery – together with the adjacent Flers Line up as far as the village of Le Sars, thus acquiring a better base for his next forward thrust.

These plans were fully in accord with Sir Douglas Haig's views, expressed the following day in a GHQ letter (OAD159) listing Fourth Army's objectives as Le Transloy, Beaulencourt, the ridge north of the Thilloy–Warlencourt valley, and Loupart Wood. This was, of course, a broad target and success naturally depended on the British overcoming points of German resistance in the intervening area. The farm at Eaucourt l'Abbaye was thought to be one such, as was Le Sars. Progress towards both had been made by the infantry on 27 September, but much remained to be done.

The date for the assault on Eaucourt and the neighbouring enemy trenches was fixed for 1 October and Zero hour for 3.15 p.m. When the attack began the New Zealand Division, a component of XV Corps, advanced in the face of heavy machine-gun fire and suffered severe casualties before finally overrunning the German strong-point known as the Circus and establishing themselves on the Le Barque road. Their losses would have been even more serious had it not been for the excellent barrage put down by the field artillery, but the gains they made here were certainly helpful to III Corps by further isolating the Germans defending the farm.

The advance by the battalions of III Corps was watched by Major J. Chammier, the commanding officer of 34 Squadron RFC, flying above the battlefield:

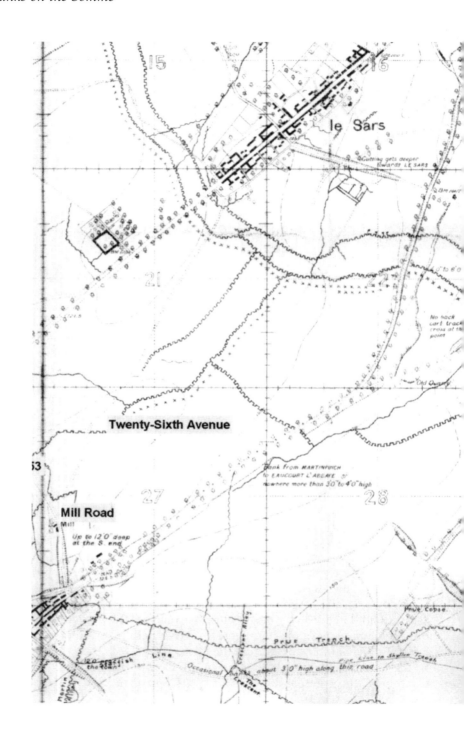

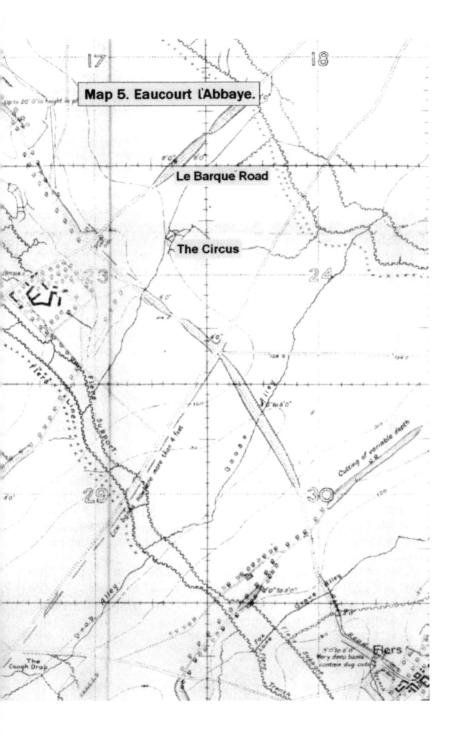

Map 5. Eaucourt l'Abbaye.

Le Barque Road

The Circus

At 3.15 p.m. the steady bombardment changed into a most magnificent barrage. The timing of this was extremely good. Guns opened simultaneously and the effect was that of many machine guns opening fire on the same order. As seen from the air the barrage appeared to be the most perfect wall of fire in which it was inconceivable that anything could live.

But the men of 47th Division's 141st Brigade,[1] south of the farm and next to the New Zealanders, soon got into trouble:

It was my impression at the time that they were having some difficulty in getting into formation for attack from their forming up places, with the result that they appeared to be very late and to be some distance behind the barrage when it lifted off the German front line at Eaucourt l'Abbaye, and immediately west of it. It was plain that here there was a good chance of failure and this actually came about, for the men had hardly advanced a couple of hundred yards, apparently, when they were seen to fall and take cover in shell holes, being presumably held up by machine gun and rifle fire.

The Londoners whom Chammier saw now waited in their shell holes for the tanks which they had been told were due to arrive. But both of these – one male and one female – had been kept back, no doubt under camouflage, at the Starfish Redoubt, not shown on map 5, the former German strong-point along the road from High Wood, and were not due to start out from there before Zero. Their route to the German front line in Flers Trench was to take them via another former redoubt, the Cough Drop, and along the north side of Drop Alley (Sachsen Weg) – in all 1100m of ground, pockmarked with shell holes and littered with debris, which they covered in 40 minutes.[2]

The machines were those of Second Lieutenant H.G.F. Bown and Lieutenant W.J. Wakley. These, together with Lieutenant H.R. Bell's (see later chapter), were allocated to III Corps under Captain G.W. Mann on 22 September. Of the three, Bown was the only commander who had already been in action. On 15 September, despite his tank having a damaged tail assembly, he had done valiant work by protecting the flank of the New Zealand Division between Longueval and High Wood – work for which he was awarded the Military Cross and during which he was temporarily blinded by glass splinters. On that occasion he had commanded the male tank D8 (720) and it was in this same machine that he found himself today. Wakley had not taken part in the earlier action, but today was in command of the female D16 (538 *Dracula*), the tank commanded on 15 September by Lieutenant A.E. Arnold.

The tanks were obviously too far behind, owing to lack of covered approaches, to be able to take part in the original attack, but they were soon seen advancing on either side of the Eaucourt l'Abbaye–Flers line, continuously in action and doing splendid work.

In its later account of these events, the III Corps War Diary gives us several timings for the progress of these tanks but does not make it clear whether these relate to each sighting or to the receipt of a report on it back at headquarters. But it seems certain that progress was good, and that the infantry waiting in the shell holes were soon able to rise up and follow the tanks on their northerly path. One of these, D8, had crossed Flers Trench at M29d 4.5 then continued over Flers Support before turning left in the direction of Eaucourt. On the way there Bown encountered isolated pockets of brave resistance but dispersed these with point-blank fire from his 6-pdr. Meanwhile D16 drove up between the two trenches before meeting up with D8 at M23c 9.1, where Bown was once more seen using his 6-pdr to good effect on the German defences around the farm enclosure. Thereafter the two tanks diverged again.

On the right, where most of the enemy opposition had been swept away, the 19th Londoners were able to swing to the east of the farm and link up with the New Zealanders along the Le Barque road. Their immediate neighbours on the left, the 20th, poured through the remains of the farm to join up with the 19th but unfortunately failed to ensure that the buildings were clear of the enemy. This was to have serious consequences, for it was now that both tanks became ditched in the Flers Line south-west of the farm. Without their support the left battalion, the 17th, already brought to a halt by uncut wire and German machine-gun fire, found itself in grave danger and, when the enemy counter-attacked down both Flers Trench and Flers Support, its men fell back. As they did so, they were fired on in enfilade by enemy forces re-emerging from the ruins of the farm and they suffered in consequence.

The two tanks were now isolated, immovable and vulnerable. D Company's War Diary says Wakley's was at M23c 2.4 and Bown's at M23c 3.7, although Bown himself later said he had ditched at M23c 5.5. Lacking infantry support, both commanders decided that to prevent their tanks falling into the hands of the enemy they should set fire to their machines and then withdraw. Bown's men escaped unscathed; Wakley and one of his men were wounded as they made their way back.

Britain's *Official History* quotes Bavarian accounts as saying that Eaucourt l'Abbaye was 'regarded as lost' on the afternoon of 1 October. It is, of course, regrettable that the tanks were unable to support the 17th Londoners beyond the farm, for this would have helped their neighbours in 50th Division attempting to capture Le Sars, but it is undoubtedly true that, without the tanks, Eaucourt l'Abbaye would have remained for some considerable time as a thorn in the side of any further British attack in this general area alongside the Albert–Bapaume road.

In his diary for this day Haig paid tribute to the German soldiers who had so bravely tackled the 'regular little fortress', which was Britain's Mark I tank.

Field Guide
IGN Map 2407E

To see the area of Starfish Redoubt, take the Rue de l'Abbaye out of the main square in Flers. The road bends round to a water-tower but just before reaching this, turn left along a road which extends well into the adjacent farmland, on its way to High Wood. Follow this past a road which bears half-right (600m from the tower) and past another (at 850m) which leads left up to the obelisk of the New Zealand Memorial. This was the eastern arm of the Fork (La Fourche). After a further 500m you reach its western arm (the portion nearer to the Memorial now, alas, ploughed under), where the Starfish Redoubt lay in the corner of the field immediately ahead of you on the left side (south) of the road to High Wood. As for the Cough Drop, this lay 300–400m due north of the Starfish. From it, Drop Alley extended north-east.

Now return to the main square in Flers and head north out of the village. After dropping down through the twisting Les Cavées, where as late as the 1980s German dug-outs could still be seen in the embankments, you arrive at Factory Corner, so-called from the sugar-beet processing plant that stood here before the First World War. Turn left here and after 1.3km you arrive at a fairly sharp right-hand bend – in fact a five-way crossroads. Park your car in the adjacent field and walk down the track leading south-west in the direction of High Wood. After 520m you are exactly in line with a line of bushes, nearer to the farm and leading up slightly to its left, which appears on the map of 1916 and which may well have helped Bown and Wakley guide their tanks to the objective. Carrying on along the track, at 650m you cross over the trench known as the Flers Support. This is where Bown crossed over the track that you are on, from south to north. After another 90m you are on Flers Trench itself, the German front line.

Further along, at 870m, you arrive at a T-junction. If you walk into the field on your left and keep strictly in line with the track forming the stem of the T, you will arrive after about 200m at the point where Drop Alley met Flers Trench and where Bown and Wakley, coming from the Cough Drop, met the first German defenders.

Should you wish to save some walking, you can reach the T-junction by car. Leave the five-way crossroads and drive up to the Eaucourt–Le Barque road, passing as you do so the Circus in the fields on your right. Now turn left, past the farm, and after 500m turn off to the left along the access road which forms the stem of the T just mentioned. It is 1km in length but follows a route slightly different from the one shown on the 1916 map. As you proceed, you will see that its first stretch provides a closer view of the places where the tanks came to a halt. An even closer vantage point can be gained by going through the area of sheds and barns of Eaucourt farm. Here, M23c 2.4 lies in the field in front of you; M23c 5.5 lies along the line of bushes extending away from you on the left, while M23c 3.7 is shrouded by the trees and new buildings of the farm.

---

[1]   The War Diary of D Company shows the division here, incorrectly, as being the 1st Division but this had been replaced by the 47th several days before.

[2]   The History of 47th Division says it took the tanks one hour.

Chapter 6

Le Sars:
7 October

On 7 October there was fierce fighting along the entire front of Fourth Army from Les Boeufs across to Le Sars but it was only in this latter place that a tank – just one – was used. The proposals for its employment, originally planned for 4 October but delayed for three days by bad weather, were outlined in III Corps' Operation Order 143 of 3 October and involved sending it against the village from the south-west in support of an assault by 23rd Division. The force chosen to work with it was 12th Battalion Durham Light Infantry, a unit of the division's 68th Brigade.

The tank was D2 (a female, 539) commanded, as it had been on 15 September, by Lieutenant H.R. Bell. On that earlier occasion he had become ditched even before reaching his start point near Delville Wood, and as a result of that (or of a subsequent incident) he had been slightly wounded. Evidently the harm to man and machine was not so grievous as to prevent them going into action again today.

Zero along the whole front was at 1.45 p.m. The attack plan called for Bell to drive his tank along the road leading north-east out of Martinpuich up to a point 825m short of Eaucourt l'Abbaye. Here at M28a 8.9 a minor track, graced by the name of the Martinpuich–Warlencourt Road, branched left. This led in turn to a point half-way along the Sunken Road linking Eaucourt l'Abbaye with Le Sars, but Bell's First Objective was the Tangle, a German trench system centred on M22a 7.9 just south of the Sunken Road. It is therefore probable that he chose to approach this across the open field on the left of the track. Indeed, the map reference given in D Company's War Diary as his start point is M22c 7.1, which is a short distance to the left of the junction. Thereafter his path to the Tangle lay due north.

The War Diary of 68th Brigade tells us that 23rd Division's Final Objective lay along a line running from M16b 9.6, which was close to the quarry in front

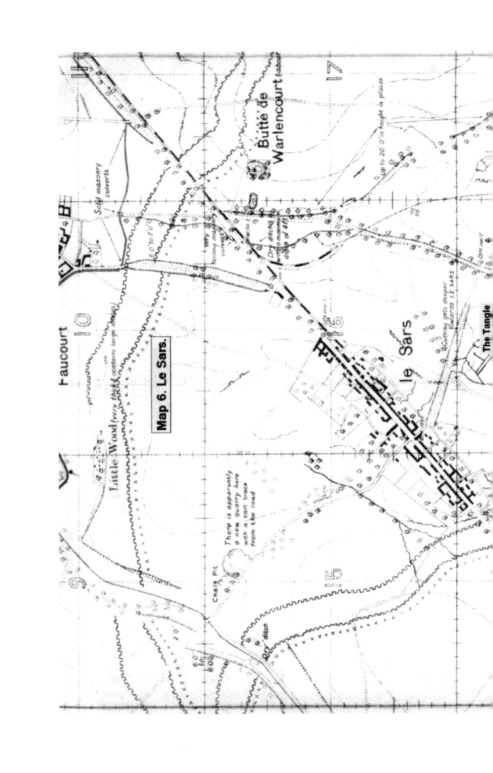

Map 6. Le Sars.

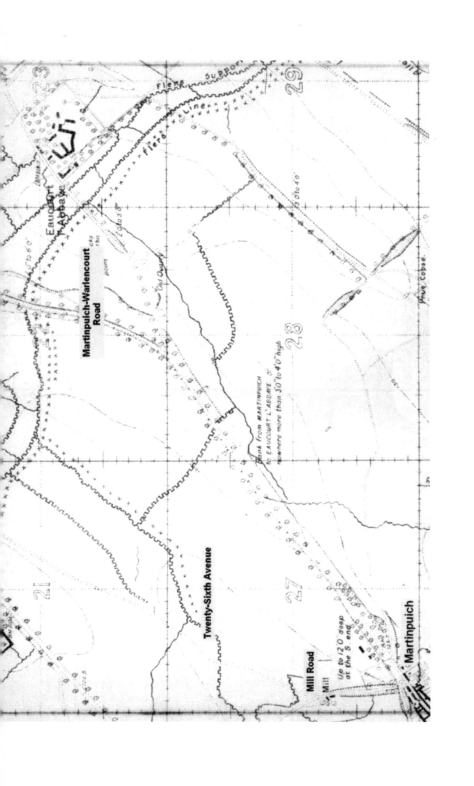

Eaucourt L'Abbaye

Martinpuich-Warlencourt Road

Flers Support Line

Flers Line

Sunken from Martinpuich to Eaucourt L'Abbaye nowhere more than 3'0" to 4'0" high

Twenty-Sixth Avenue

Mill Road

Mill

Up to 12'0 deep at the 'S' end

Martinpuich

of the Butte de Warlencourt, then through M16a 7.4 near the northernmost corner of Le Sars, then over to the crossroads at M9c 7.0 – all of which meant capturing the whole village.[1] Bell's own task, after destroying the enemy in the Tangle, was to proceed west along the Sunken Road and help the 12th Durham Light Infantry enter the built-up area. He started on time, successfully cleared the Tangle, then turned his attention to the village. Unfortunately he was now too obvious a target and a German shell disabled his machine. As they got out, three members of the crew were wounded, either by high explosive shell or by shrapnel. Bell was unhurt but his tank caught fire and was destroyed.

Its position was later variously reported by at least four observers, two showing it south of the road and two north of it. Although all four are grouped in an area no more than 90m across, only one of these identifications can be said to be accurate – M16c 7.1. In fact, an aerial photograph[2] shows it even more precisely as M16c 78.08, indicating that, instead of proceeding up the Sunken Road towards the crossroads formed by the main Albert–Bapaume highway, Bell chose to cross over it, perhaps with the intention of helping the attacking force by destroying any enemy emplacements found lining the southern edge of the village.

The 12th Durham Light Infantry were held up here for a little while longer by machine-gun fire from the crossroads on the Martinpuich–Warlencourt Road, but they and the 13th Battalion later continued the fight, together with other units, and by the end of the day the enemy had been driven out of the village entirely. The *Official History* rightly considered this 'a striking success' and praised Bell's 'excellent service' in helping to achieve it.[3]

Field Guide

IGN Map 2407E

At the north-east end of Martinpuich, take the road leading straight out of the village, avoiding the one which turns north up to the main Albert–Bapaume highway. After 1.4km there is a rough track leading half-left. In 1916 this was known as the Martinpuich–Warlencourt Road. In the field to the left of this junction was Bell's start point. The track itself formed the boundary between 23rd Division on the west and 47th Division on the east.

It is not advisable to take your car up the track, so carry on to the farm of Eaucourt l'Abbaye and turn left towards Le Sars. The crossroads where the road and track intersect was the place from where German machine gunners fired on the British infantry and no doubt also on D2.

After 200m an asphalted road leads left, as shown on the trench map of 1916. Roughly in the far corner of the junction, on your left, was the Tangle.

At a point 100m further on there was once a tree-lined path leading into the field on your right. On the far side of this, only 20m from the road, is where D2 was brought to a halt.

1   The last reference given in the Diary is M15a 7.10, but this is invalid. The sense, however, is clear; it refers to the crossroads at the coordinate given above, M9c 7.0, this being on the road to Pys.

2   IWM photograph 34c530, Box 161, dated 20 October 1916.

3   Lieutenant, later Major, Hugh Reginald Bell of 11th Battalion of the Tank Corps died on 3 September 1918 and is buried in Grave K3, Plot VIII, Cabaret Rouge Military Cemetery, Souchez, north of Arras. He had been educated at St Paul's School and Magdalen College, Oxford. He was killed by a chance shell when leading a group of four tanks through the village of Harcourt on the Arras–Cambrai road.

Chapter 7

Bayonet Trench:
18 October

The attack on 18 October against Bayonet Trench and an adjacent length of the Gird Line was, like other operations in this sector, part of Fourth Army's response to Haig's OAD 159 of 29 September in which he set out his targets for forthcoming offensive action. The places specified included villages on the Transloy Ridge to the east as well as the high ground north of Ligny-Thilloy and Warlencourt, all of which lay between 3 and 5km beyond the positions north of Flers where the action took place that we are about to describe. Progress towards them had, of course, been made, albeit slowly and at great cost, as part of the battles being waged since the very outset of the Somme offensive. More recently, substantial portions of the Gird Line – the two parallel trenches of Gird Trench itself and Gird Support – had been captured by 55th Division on 27 September, but the all-important junction of these with Goose Alley had remained in enemy hands despite gallant assaults by the neighbouring New Zealand Division's 1st Otago Regiment. A further attack on the 28th by the under-strength 1st Wellington and by two companies of 4th Rifles was cancelled when a tank which was due to support them failed to arrive.

The reason for its non-appearance is not given in the official records, nor is the name of its commander, but the diary kept by D Company's adjutant mentions that Lieutenant H.G. Head, one of the officers whose tank had been due to accompany Storey's in its attack on the Gird Line on the 25th (see earlier chapter), was prevented from doing so by a broken track. Following repair, the machine was re-allocated late on the 26th for an attack to be mounted elsewhere, apparently on the 27th. The sector where it was to operate is not specified but we think it must have been this machine that the New Zealanders were expecting to assist them, not in their main action on the 27th for which it was too late, but in the resumed operation arranged for

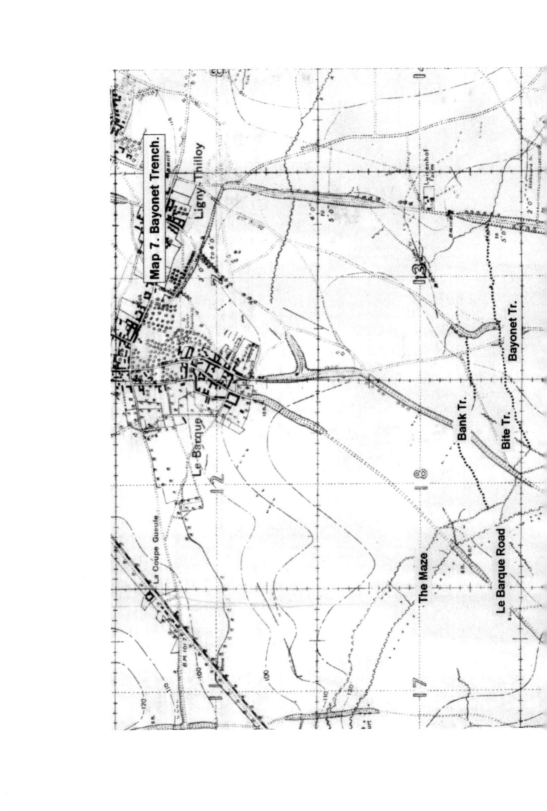

Map 7. Bayonet Trench.

Ligny-Thilloy

Le Barque

La Coupe Gueule

The Maze

Le Barque Road

Bank Tr.

Bite Tr.

Bayonet Tr.

Luisenhof Farm

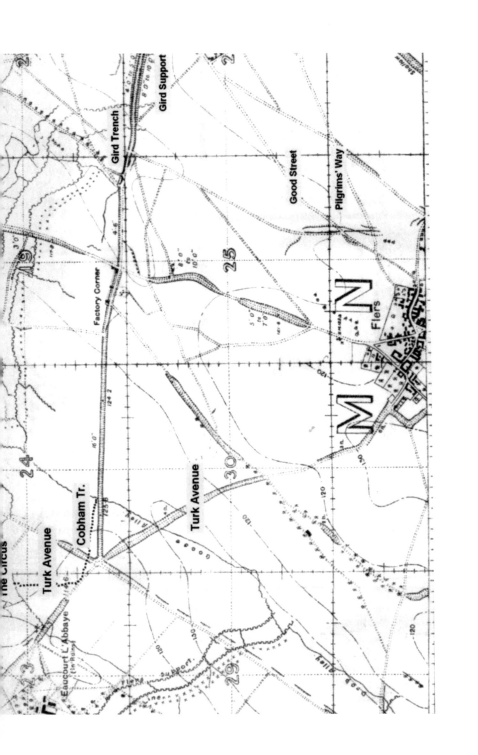

the following day. However, for some reason Head was 'withdrawn' before he reached their lines. The frustration of the New Zealand liaison officer, waiting in vain in the dead of night at the rendezvous near Factory Corner, can easily be imagined, for neither he nor his divisional commander had been kept informed of Head's whereabouts. Head was a gallant officer, whose action on the 15th had earned him the MC. Having been ditched north of Delville Wood on that day, his machine – D3, a male, no. 728 – had been recovered on the 18th and, as we say, it must have been this same machine that the New Zealanders were now waiting for in the early hours of the 28th.

We know, of course, that progress in this area was made later, on 1 October, by the New Zealanders and 47th Division – this latter now aided by tanks – in the area of Eaucourt l'Abbaye. Further attacks were carried out by 41st Division on 7 October, the day when Bell took part in the assault on nearby Le Sars, and these advanced the line a few hundred metres beyond Gird Support, but efforts made by 30th Division on 12 October – just a day after it took over from the 41st – left the line much as it had been.

On 13 October an order was issued by Rawlinson's headquarters calling on his three Corps Commanders to prepare new plans for an attack all along the Fourth Army front, when tanks would be made available if they could be used to advantage. He also expressed the view that the attacks might be best carried out at night, an idea which he had put forward for the initial offensive on 15 September but which had been rejected by Haig – and by Ernest Swinton when writing on tactics several months before! Just why Rawlinson chose to resurrect it now, when the weather made conditions even less favourable, is hard to understand. In the event, the attack on 18 October certainly began in total darkness at 3.40 a.m.

In XV Corps, meetings of senior officers were held on 15 October to study the means whereby an attacking force could break through the main barrier now facing it in the shape of Bayonet Trench, which extended in a broad arc beyond the British front line north-west of Flers. Attending these meetings were the new commander of XV Corps, Lieutenant-General J.P. du Cane, and the commander of 30th Division, Major-General J.S.M. Shea. Also taking part was Captain A.M. Inglis of HSMGC (Heavy Section Machine Gun Corps), brought in to advise on the best way of using the tanks soon to be allocated to the attack. He was an officer of C Company, but the tanks and their commanders were from D Company – not surprisingly, since this part of the front had hitherto fallen within D Company's area of responsibility.

At noon on the 16th a further conference was held at Viviers Mill, south of Albert, when it was announced that recent aircraft reconnaissance had revealed the existence of a new German defence line, later called Bank Trench, constructed behind Bayonet Trench. This news came as an unpleasant surprise to Shea as it meant urgent modification of the tactical plan already cleared with du Cane and explained orally to Brigadier-General R.W. Morgan, the commander of 21st Brigade, which was the formation chosen to mount the attack. In the end it was decided to treat an assault on the new, more distant, trench as a separate operation.

As nothing had yet been put on paper about all this, steps were quickly taken during the night of 16th/17th to remedy the omission. 30th Division's Operational Order 42 and other documents were completed for signature by 3.15 a.m. but were not issued to Signals until 8.15 a.m. They were then entrusted to a Captain Bury to take to 21st Brigade HQ near Flers. Morgan, however, later claimed that he had received no new orders until the afternoon of the 17th. This clearly allowed very little time for him to issue his own orders to battalion commanders, or for them to issue theirs to their own subordinate units, so even before knowing what precisely was required of them, some of these simply issued what instructions they thought might in the circumstances be useful. This, of course, was no substitute for properly drafted and carefully coordinated planning. Inevitably, there was considerable confusion about lines of advance, objectives, consolidation and follow-on action.

The problems thus caused were made worse by an order which Morgan received – presumably by telephone, for there is no written copy that we have seen – telling him to withdraw all his men from the front trenches that same afternoon in order to allow a bombardment of the German lines from 2.00 to 5.00 p.m. He argued strongly against this withdrawal but the order was confirmed, albeit with a reduction from three to two hours. There followed scenes of great confusion as men hurried to the rear along the communication trenches. Later, as they were still returning to reoccupy the front line, a retaliatory German bombardment came crashing down on Goose Alley, one of those same crowded communication trenches. In the circumstances it is not surprising that battalion officers found it almost impossible to issue any orders at all to the men under their command.

To add to the British concerns, threatening clouds now began to blot out the sun. Shea had already made a point of waking at hourly intervals in the night of 15th/16th in order to check on the weather, but apart from a few showers it had practically stopped raining several days before then and he must have been heartened to see the moon shining brightly in a starlit sky. The result on the 16th was a crisp and clear day which repeated itself when dawn broke on the 17th. But would this drier spell hold until the 18th?

It was probably on the 16th (although the date is not clear on the original document) that 30th Division published its G.419, which said that three tanks would be taking part in the operation. All of these, after leaving Flers, were to proceed along Abbey Road, then halt at a point near 21st Brigade headquarters at M30c 3.1, where they would be given final instructions, for it had been decided that they would only go into battle if the infantry attack failed.

If they were indeed called forward, the tanks would approach their battle positions via Turk Avenue and the five-way crossroads half-way between Factory Corner and Eaucourt l'Abbaye. From here two of the tanks would cross Cobham Trench and proceed via the track leading north then head for a point shown as M18d 1.1. This was described as being on the German front line but in fact it lay on Gird Support, the more distant of the two Gird trenches. Nearby was the German strong-point known as the Maze, which was clearly going to cause major problems for the advancing infantry.

At the five-way crossroads the third machine was to have turned north-west to join the road leading from Eaucourt towards Le Barque, then follow this into no-man's-land and attack three enemy machine guns thought to be sited in a trench well forward of the Gird Line at M18c 3.3.

In the event only two tanks took part in the attack, neither of which followed this latter route. We do not know when this change of plan was announced, but we do know that a group of three tank subalterns, almost certainly accompanied by Inglis, at some stage on the 16th reconnoitred the ground in front of Bayonet Trench in preparation for the attack. It would seem, however, that one of the three was soon afterwards assigned to work instead with the neighbouring 12th Division on the right.

At 6 p.m. on the 17th the scene that they had all surveyed the day before was about to change for the worse. The rain fell gently at first, then gradually increased in intensity until it was pouring down in torrents. The men in the trenches were soon soaked to the skin and bitterly cold, as well as being tired from their enforced earlier withdrawal. The ground, which had earlier improved with the dry weather, now returned to its former marshy condition, soft and slippery underfoot, the myriad shell-holes now filling with water and slime. It was going to be hard enough to stand up, let alone advance in the dark against a determined enemy. Mud was everywhere, not least in the trenches where rain-soaked clothing became caked with it, and where even the men's rifles became clogged and useless. Until shortly before Zero the moon was blanketed by thick cloud, which made the decision to set Zero for 3.40 a.m. seem with hindsight to be almost bizarre.

In assembly positions separated from the Germans to the north by a strip of ground varying between 65 and 180m wide, three battalions of British infantry stood in the dark, the cold and the rain, waiting for Zero. Morgan had placed 2nd Yorkshire Regiment (Green Howards) on the right, 18th King's (Liverpool) Regiment in the centre and 2nd Wiltshire Regiment on the left. The 19th Manchester Regiment was held in reserve. The whole brigade had but one task – to attack and hold just one segment of the enemy line measuring

900m long, from N13c 20.25 in Bayonet Trench to M18c 60.75 in Gird Support. The requirement to advance further, and to capture the newly discovered Bank Trench lying beyond Bayonet Trench, was, as agreed earlier, ignored, although the map issued with 30th Division's Operational Order 68 of 16 October had certainly shown this as the Objective.

At Zero, the Yorkshiremen on the right seemed at first to make relatively good progress and were well over half-way to the German trenches before a shower of grenades fell upon them. Nothing daunted, they re-formed and continued the advance for a while before finally losing heart. Their officers had become casualties and, without leadership at this critical moment, just when success seemed within their grasp, they faltered, and the survivors simply returned as best they could to their own lines.

It is worth noting that the attacking Yorkshiremen may have been deceived by a trick. A British artillery observer reported that at one stage the rockets used by the Germans for signalling to their command posts in the rear were no longer being fired from Bayonet Trench, suggesting that the men defending it had withdrawn or had been overwhelmed. Instead, red flares of the kind used by the attacking British infantry to indicate their own forward positions were seen there. Several possible explanations for this spring to mind. Perhaps the attackers *did* get into the trench, although no mention of this is to be found in the Yorkshires' own very detailed account. On the contrary, this tells us that the attack halted when several yards from the trench. Or perhaps the artillery observer was mistaken. Alternatively, the Germans used red flares to deceive the attackers into thinking that some of their own men had captured the trench and that they could now advance over the open to join them, only to be shot down as they did so. The reader may think this an unlikely scenario but it is precisely what happened to men of the East Yorkshire Regiment and King's Own Yorkshire Light Infantry just five weeks before in a portion of Gird Trench south-east of Gueudecourt.[1]

Despite this check to the main advance, a party of Yorkshire bombers under Lieutenant R.A. Field made good initial progress up Bite Trench but many of these, too, later became casualties, mainly by fire from a so-called X Trench. This had recently been dug by the Germans between Bite Trench and the Maze and the bombers had a hard time alternately attacking the enemy and sheltering from his return fire.

In the centre of the British attack there was an early loss of direction among the King's and this was in part to blame for their failure, but uncut wire on their right and fierce opposition from the Maze strong-point behind it were additional problems. Also morale was low among men soaked to the skin, cold, weary and made nervous by earlier 'shorts' from their own artillery. Some of them, new to the fighting but who had managed to reach the German line, were reluctant to jump down into the enemy's trenches despite repeated efforts to persuade them to do so. Dispirited, they began to fall back to their lines only half an hour after setting out.

On the left the Wiltshires, who had suffered badly from shell fire even as they moved up from the rear the previous evening, nevertheless attacked in fine form but were soon lost to view in the darkness and mist. Thereafter, little was heard from the foremost waves in C and D Companies and it was thought that they must have entered the German lines – which indeed was the case, according to one or two returning wounded – or else that they had pushed on further. The lack of more precise news was thought at first to be a good sign, although when a runner, followed later by an officer, was sent ahead to discover the reason, their failure to return caused disquiet. Only much later did it transpire that some of the attacking parties had lost direction and strayed over the sunken Le Barque road into the sector of the neighbouring division, while others had crossed over Gird Trench only to be killed or captured by the enemy in Gird Support. In all, sixty men were missing.[2]

It was, however, his receipt at 4.16 a.m. of news that the 18th King's were already back in their trenches that prompted Morgan to call forward his two tanks. In the mistaken belief that the Wiltshires were succeeding where the other battalions were not, he ruled that the tank which he had ordered to advance on the left, where the Wiltshires were, should instead stay in the centre, where the Maze was holding out against the King's.

During daylight on the 17th the two tanks in question – two out of the three originally proposed – had left their rear base at the Loop, near Bray, and headed for their forward base at Green Dump, south-west of Longueval.[3] After dark, they continued on to Flers where they found what shelter they could. It had been thought that on a clear night any advance further forward would be given away by sparks from the tanks' exhausts, but in the event the rain and the mist would have allowed them to proceed undiscovered. Progress, however, was made painfully slow by the quagmire now everywhere encountered, which makes it all the more surprising that they left it as late as 2.40 a.m. before setting out again from their temporary stopping-place in or near the village. For it was only at Zero hour, 3.40 a.m., that Inglis – who had evidently now stationed himself at 21st Brigade HQ – reported to the staff there that the tanks had resumed their onward march an hour before. They may well have done so, but in that hour they had still not covered the distance to the HQ dug-out – no more than 900m if they had been stationed near the northern exit of the village, but considerably more if they had chosen a place closer to the more sheltered southern end, the ruins and wreckage later encountered no doubt adding to the time necessary for the journey.

It was at 6.30 a.m. that one of the machines, the male, arrived near the brigade dug-out, which lay 365m west of the tanks' approach route along Abbey Road. The second, the female, stayed languishing back in Flers, evidently suffering from mechanical problems. It was still there when the male left brigade headquarters at 7 a.m. This was much later than hoped, the delay made worse by an unexplained second pause by the male only a short distance further on. Perhaps the officer had decided to wait for his female companion to catch up with him, or perhaps he had encountered technical problems of his own. Whatever the cause, he only resumed progress about 7.20 a.m. and did not pass the British front line until 8.04 a.m. This was *very* much later than hoped for, because Morgan had been told that it would be there at 5.30 a.m. Believing that once the tanks got into action there would be little hostile opposition, he had ordered the infantry, with the exception of those engaged around the Maze and Bite Trench, to await the arrival of the tanks before mounting further attacks, so a lengthy hiatus ensued.

But at long last the male reached Gird Trench at M24a 9.6. The subsequent report by 30th Division reads:

> There he sat for 23 minutes and achieved good success against the enemy bolting up the communication trench, particularly along the road through M24a, where about fifty casualties were caused. He also destroyed a German machine gun. The officer in charge got out of the tank and signalled to the infantry to come on. It would seem that a good opportunity was lost here, but at this time the regiments were very much mixed up and communication along our front trenches was quite impossible even if their own officers, most of whom had been knocked out, had been there to re-organise. The tank then went along the front line to M18c 4.7, with the Germans running before him. He stopped there ten minutes emptying the trenches and then returned to 21st Brigade headquarters, where he arrived about 10 a.m. considerably knocked about and not fit to make another effort. [*But he*] had seen nothing of the party of Wiltshires, which up to that time were confidently believed to be consolidating its first objective.

A second version of this action, quoting the officer in command of the tank, was given in 21st Brigade's War Diary:

> He crossed our front line just east of the track in M24a and remained stationary on Gird Trench opposite this point for 23 minutes. Germans ran back along Gird Support Trench and got out on to the road running north-east through M18d where he killed a good many with his machine guns. He then turned north-west and went along the back of Gird Trench as far as M18c 5.7 where he turned south-west and came back along the northern side of the [Eaucourt–Le Barque] Sunken Road. He saw none of our troops in Gird Trench but observed them in the Sunken Road and in a trench running parallel to it on its southern side. His action was evidently of great assistance to the troops attacking on our left and I

consider that the work of this officer was most excellent. He did not, however, actually get into the Maze, nor did his action dispose of the resistance to our bombing parties along the south-eastern face of the Maze.

The Maze would, of course, have been dealt with by the female tank, had it been present, but it was not until 8.40 a.m. that, having apparently rectified whatever problem had plagued it in Flers, it finally passed brigade HQ on its way to the forward lines, where it arrived about 10 a.m. The 30th Division account says of this machine:

> The intention was that she should cooperate with the 19th Manchesters [*hitherto in reserve*] in a renewed attack. The tank was to cross our front line at the same place as her consort had done, but to move eastwards and subdue resistance in the Maze, which would have enabled our bombers to get on. Unfortunately the tank stuck behind our front line and its advance never materialised so that the intended renewal never took place. In view of the impossibility of reorganising before nightfall it was decided to make no second attack unaided by a tank.

Morgan wrote:

> On hearing that the second tank was able to get forward, I directed O.C. 19th Manchester Regiment to relieve 18th King's (Liverpool) Regiment and to make the same attack in conjunction with the second tank. At 10.30 a.m. the Brigade Major was sent up to ascertain the situation in our own trenches and explain the scheme of attack to the commanding officers concerned. This tank, however, stuck behind our line at about M24b 3.2 and was unable to move.

He then went on:

> Exact instructions as to the movements of this tank had been given to the officer [*Captain Inglis*] in charge of the two tanks at Brigade headquarters, but on my Brigade Major going to see the officer actually in command of the second tank, he discovered that this officer was provided with a very incorrect map and that his instructions did not tally with those which had been given to the officer [*Inglis*] at Brigade headquarters. Consequently he went too far to the east instead of crossing our front line at the same point as the first one and then bearing eastwards to deal with the Maze. As I considered that an infantry attack with the force at my disposal was quite impracticable unless aided by a tank, this last attack by 19th Manchester Regiment was not made . . . Had the tanks been able to advance so as to take part in a second attack just as dawn was breaking, I am convinced that the first objective at any rate might have been captured.

The implied criticism of Inglis made here is obviously serious. There may be an explanation for what he did, or rather what he was accused of having done, but we have no record of what this could have been. Perhaps he had learned that the route specified by the brigade had become too hazardous, or that the plight of infantry elsewhere had suddenly become too pressing for him to follow instructions laid down by headquarters staff some distance in the rear. But only in rare circumstances do officers contravene orders issued from on high, and if Inglis had grounds for wanting to modify his instructions he should have got word back to the brigadier explaining his thinking. After all, the place where he must have briefed the commander of the second tank – Abbey Road – was only 365m from brigade headquarters. A quick discussion of his new ideas with Morgan would have taken no more than ten or fifteen minutes, possibly much less.

We must bear in mind, however, that Inglis was a brave and resourceful officer who did well on 15 September, fighting at the Courcelette Sugar Factory in his tank C5, *Crème de Menthe* – an action for which he was awarded the Distinguished Service Order, and for which he received a personal commendation from the commander of the 2nd Canadian Division with which he was working. He also did well at Thiepval if, as we assume to be the case, he was again in command of *Crème de Menthe,* which did valuable service at the chateau there on 26 September (see later chapter).

There is an odd postscript to this incident in the War Diary of C Company, where an entry dated 23 October 1916 reads: 'Report received from Captain Inglis on the work of tanks attached to XIV, XV and III Corps'. This entry, and indeed the whole War Diary, was almost certainly written by C Company's adjutant, Captain R.E. Williams, who added the note 'Appx XII' in the adjacent column reserved for the reference number of any attachment accompanying the Diary. That note was then deleted by Major Allen Holford-Walker (the brother of Archie Holford-Walker), who placed his initials against the deletion. Moreover, he must have deleted it as soon as he saw it because the XII serial number was then allocated instead to the immediately following item. But if he had wished to conceal the existence of the report he should perhaps have deleted the whole entry or, better, started a new sheet. It was, after all, only the second entry on the sheet.[4]

Also missing from the files are pages 7 and 8 of 30th Division's account of the battle, which at its end saw all the survivors of the attack back in the same trenches from which they had emerged at Zero. On pages 9 and 10 of this account the cause of their failure was blamed largely on the weather, this being about as hostile to the British as was the enemy opposite. Plans had been laid on the assumption of a moonlit night, dry for the most part, just as it had been on several preceding nights. Instead, thick cloud and cold, heavy rain beforehand had made the operation a nightmare. Even though the rain had stopped some time before Zero, its effect on the ground, on the men's morale and on their weapons was all too evident.

Also responsible, in the view of 30th Division, was the time taken to get out orders, and indeed one senses an element of dithering, leading to delay, then panic, in the way that XV Corps formulated and issued its instructions. 30th Division's account reads:

> Battalion orders were issued before brigade orders. Brigade orders were at divisional headquarters before divisional orders were issued. It was not possible to issue divisional orders until after the conference on the afternoon of the 16th . . . Corps orders did not reach the division until well on in the morning of the 18th . . . Had the division waited to write orders until after the receipt of corps orders, the companies in the front line would never have got orders at all. The earlier issue of higher formation orders would be greatly appreciated if this could possibly be arranged.

One hopes that the restrained criticism in this last sentence was not lost on Lieutenant-General du Cane, who had taken over command of XV Corps less than three weeks before. He had never had a field command, having earlier been a staff officer with III Corps, then an artillery adviser at GHQ, and latterly at the Ministry of Munitions in London.

And what about the tanks? Did they share any blame? Well, certainly the officer who took the male tank along the German lines and in vain urged on the infantry – an action which earned him an individual (albeit anonymous) mention in Britain's *Official History* – must be beyond criticism. As for his companion in the female tank which became stuck, we must reserve judgement, but we know that these first tanks were subject to a number of mechanical problems and also that deep mud was as much their enemy as were the Germans.

So was Inglis to blame? He is accused of having mis-directed the female tank, but it is doubtful if this one machine, on its own, would have been any more successful in encouraging the infantry forward than was its predecessor.

It would have helped us to resolve the question if Holford-Walker had not destroyed the original Appendix XII in his War Diary, and if we knew what was in those missing pages 7 and 8 in 30th Division's report on the battle. The suspicion must be that Inglis' own report contained a frank explanation of his decision to amend the tankman's orders and therefore some criticism, implied or explicit, of his superiors' judgement when planning the attack. If this conjecture is correct, then Holford-Walker's action in suppressing it may have been prompted by a wish not to offend the new commander of XV Corps, Lieutenant-General du Cane. Or was he piqued that a mere captain in his company had presumed to write an account of which he, as the commander of Inglis's company, or Major Summers as the commander of the men involved, would have been a more appropriate author? The only objection to that idea is that for most of the period Holford-Walker and Summers were fully engaged north of the Ancre in helping to organise a large operation planned by Reserve Army, and had been far removed from the action at Bayonet Trench.

One sad aspect of this whole episode is that assistance was offered to 30th Division by its neighbour on the right, 12th Division, who proposed lending them their own tank to help the infantry forward. Only later did 12th Division discover that the tank in question was still at Green Dump, almost 5km to the rear, undergoing repair.

Finally, can we make a guess as to the identity of the three tank officers chosen to operate in this area? Well, we have already said that they were probably from D Company, even though the officer commanding them locally was Captain Inglis, from C Company. It is A.F. Becke's admirable *Order of Battle* that tells us this, but he does not name them. However, a reference in D Company's War Diary provides a clue. Concluding the entries covering the whole period from the end of September to mid-November, during which time the bulk of D Company's tanks were positioned near Beaumont Hamel, the diarist says, 'During these operations north of the Ancre there were three officers – Lieutenants Head, Hastie and Pearsall – commanded by Captain Inglis DSO, working from Green Dump.' The purpose of their presence in this area is not spelt out but Green Dump was the base near Longueval from which all the tanks operating against Flers had been stationed in September. Evidently it was still used for this trio, detached from the rest of D Company.

An entry in the personal diary kept by Captain Graham Woods also mentions that Head and Hastie were 'in action' on the 18th but does not say where. It would seem, however, that these two were the officers working with 30th Division, while Pearsall was the one whose role with 12th Division was ruled out by the need to repair his machine back at Green Dump.[5] Just which of the other two was in the male tank and which in the female on this day is a question that baffled us for a long time, but the position is made clearer in a paper in the National Archives[6] written by General Sir Hugh Elles to the Official Historian in 1934. After Flers-Courcelette, Elles had commanded the Tank Corps throughout the remainder of the war and presumably had access to all the documents describing these actions.

Despite this, there are a number of errors in his account, when perhaps he was relying more on his personal recollections of eighteen years before rather than on documentary proof. His main error is in saying that *five* tanks were engaged in the fight for Bayonet Trench, whereas we believe that there were only three – the three mentioned in D Company's War Diary – of which only two reached the battlefield. The extra two referred to by Elles – C19 *Clan Leslie* (705), and C7 (760) – were at this time north of the Ancre, beyond Beaumont Hamel.[7]

We can, however, readily accept his identification of the male tank as D3 (728), the same machine that Head had taken into battle north of Delville Wood on 15 September, but which had ditched alongside the Longueval–Flers road, only to be recovered three days later. We are as sure as we can be that Head was again in command of this tank when it advanced along the German lines on 18 October.

We are less sure about Elles's identification of the female tank which he says was C20, factory number 533. In fact the company designation C20 was that of tank 523 (commanded on 15 September at the Quadrilateral by Lieutenant George Macpherson, and on 25–27 September at Morval by Lieutenant Sir John Dashwood). The factory number 533 on the other hand belonged to tank C22 (commanded on 15 September at the Quadrilateral by Lieutenant Basil Henriques). Although they had each sustained damage in that earlier fighting, at least one of these – either C20 or C22 – was evidently thought fit to fight again in the action at Bayonet Trench, but the problems now besetting it on the way up were obviously of a serious order according to Elles, who said it was 'unable to assist the infantry owing to a breakdown of steering, loose tracks, and finally ditching in a shell hole'. The unfortunate commander of this female tank must have been Hastie but at least he had won fame on 15 September when his earlier tank, D17 *Dinnaken*, was described in RFC reports, and subsequently acclaimed in the British press, as having 'walked down the High Street of Flers with the British Army cheering behind'.

And the third member of the trio, left behind at Green Dump? That can only have been Second Lieutenant Pearsall, whose D11, *Die Hard*, had been the only tank to see action on both 15 and 16 September, but was now left a wreck on the road north of Flers. The identity of his tank on 18 October is not known.

The *Official History* summed up the operation as follows:

Two tanks, held in readiness at Flers, were to be used if the night assault failed. At 8 a.m., when the fighting had died down, one machine crossed the British front line and sat at the end of Gird Trench for twenty minutes doing great execution amongst the Germans, who fled back north-eastward. The tank commander climbed out and signalled for the infantry to come on, but the front was so disorganised, the men so exhausted, and the number of officers so few, that no response was possible. Driving the enemy before it, the tank then went forward alone along Gird Trench as far as the Le Barque road, and then retired by the way that it had come. The second tank found the mud too great a handicap and never reached the front line.[8]

For his part, Haig wrote in his diary at the end of the day:

> Results of the attack by Fourth Army at 3.45 a.m. were meagre. A tank moved out along the German trenches, demoralised and killed a good many Germans without the infantry taking advantage of it. The tank returned safely.

One is left wondering if the Commander-in-Chief was aware of the confusion which had evidently reigned in du Cane's corps headquarters before the battle.

Turning away for a moment from the British version of events, let us look at how one German saw the battle. *Vizefeldwebel* Tauscher of 9th Company, 104th Infantry Regiment, was a witness to the fighting at Bayonet Trench and sent his report on the tank to higher command:

> Shape: It is very elongated, not tubby nor shaped like an egg. The bow projects noticeably ahead of the wheels. The side surfaces of the body are vertical and are not curved; the rear end is also flat and is closed by means of a door. One of the members of the crew left the vehicle, walked for a short time behind it and got back in. Below the body there are fixed sledge-runners which project on the right and left ahead of the wheels. The front wheels are between 1.50 and 1.70m high, and are located in approximately the first third of the body. The rims are not flat but have projections on them so that from the side they look like cog-wheels. If one wheel slips into a shell hole or if the vehicle drives over a trench (it easily crossed a very deep sap 1.50m wide) then the vehicle rests on the runners and the wheel or the rear-wheels push the body, resting as it is on the tracks, far enough forward for the driving wheels to be able to grip again.
>
> Rear wheel: Reportedly the vehicle has only one rear wheel, which is located under the body and is equipped with spuds which give it purchase on the ground.
>
> Steering: Nothing is known about the method of steering. No trail-spade was seen on the vehicle.
>
> The way in which the drive is transferred to the wheels was not apparent from the outside. Tracks were not seen. The noise noticeable when the thing is moving is not as great as that of one of our lorries.
>
> The speed was very limited. 'It crawled like a snail.' The Englishman who got out of it could easily keep up with it.
>
> Armour: All attempts to damage the wheels with hand-grenades were in vain. No loopholes were seen.
>
> Armament and operation: Guns to the right and left in casemates like swallows' nests right in the middle of the body. At least six machine guns of which two can fire to the front and two to the rear. The guns fired shrapnel, which exploded close above the German trenches. The vehicle

crossed the first German trenches and then, trundling along between the first and second trenches, it covered the trenches with gun and machine gun fire, causing very heavy losses to the troops in them. It is reported that by this one vehicle alone three companies were put completely out of action. British infantry followed the vehicle and occupied the position.

Tauscher's unit was in position on the far north-eastern side of the Le Barque road so he must have had a fairly good view of the tank towards the end of its advance. His report and drawings were evidently brought to the immediate attention of the German High Command and were circulated in a paper on tanks issued on 21 October over the signature of General Hermann von Kuhl, Chief of Staff of Crown Prince Rupprecht's Army Group. Other versions of the 'tricycle' drawing were similarly circulated until more accurate accounts finally prevailed.[9]

Field Guide

IGN Map 2407E

The two tanks due to support 21st Brigade spent the early part of the night of 17/18 October in or near Flers, although the exact spot is not known. Hastie's machine, as we have seen, had serious mechanical problems but D3 went on ahead. Its route lay down Abbey Road but whether it reached this by travelling via *Rue de l'Abbaye* in the village or went through the open fields to the west, we do not know. We assume the former, so keeping the water-tower on your left, go down to the crossroads 700m further on, then park your car and walk along the grass track leading left. After 200m you arrive end-on at the beginning of an embankment where the track divides. The left branch of the fork leads gradually upwards onto the top of the embankment but the right-hand one takes you along its base.[10] This is the one to take, for after another 100m – opposite one of several dense clumps of shrubs lining the embankment – you are standing where Morgan had his headquarters. It lay somewhere behind the wall of vegetation on your left, and is where Inglis came to receive the Brigadier's instructions to the tank commanders. We hope the Brigadier was induced to walk back to the crossroads to wish Head and his crew good luck in the fighting. He evidently did not do this for Hastie or he would surely have learned about the new instructions which he had been given by Inglis.

From the crossroads the tanks would have taken the track (Turk Avenue) which rises alongside a row of poplars and leads to the five-way crossroads which we have already described. From here, walk up the rough track leading north. After 600m the path, such as it is, comes to an abrupt end. Turn right and walk for 200m and you will see 100–150m ahead of you a gentle rise. This is possibly where Hastie was brought to a halt. In the report later submitted by Morgan and quoted above, the point of this tank's demise is given as M24b 3.2, but an aerial photograph[11] taken on 16 November seems to show it slightly more precisely as M24b 23.05, lying across, or even in, a much damaged trench near its junction with the Germans' former Gird Trench. We have to admit that the image is not clear, possibly because the tank was half-buried in mud and surrounded by myriad shell holes.

This lack of landmarks makes it difficult to give precise directions to a visitor to the area, but one point is easy to identify. Head's progress along Gird Trench appears to have ended where this met the Eaucourt–Le Barque road. To find this, walk or drive for 900m from the Eaucourt 'crossroads' (the northern branch of which is no more than a rough track) to a large upright steel girder, placed here no doubt as some sort of boundary marker, but unrelated to the battlefield of 1916.

---

[1] For an account of this and other infantry and tank actions in 1916, see the author's *Flers and Gueudecourt* (2002).[5]   This was a new machine, his original tank D11 (*Die Hard*) having been destroyed on the road north of Flers on 16 September.

[2] *The History of the 2nd Battalion Wiltshire Regiment* by W.S. Shepherd puts the casualty figure as high as 14 officers and 350 other ranks. We cannot explain this discrepancy.

[3] Order G.419 of 16 October says the tanks were to arrive in Flers during the night of 16th/17th, then stay in Flers during the daylight hours. But other details in this Order were later altered and we believe that the timings may have been altered too.

[4] The missing Appendix does not appear in the folder of various documents retained by Allen Holford-Walker after the war which is now in the National Army Museum. The folder does, however, contain the letter of commendation referred to in the text. It reads:

> To Captain Inglis, Commanding no. 1 Section, Heavy Section, Machine Gun Corps:
>
> The G.O.C. has asked me to express to you personally, and through you to all ranks under your command, his appreciation of the work done by them during the operations last week. The ready cooperation and magnificent support which you afforded the Division was in a large measure responsible for the successes gained. The G.O.C. hopes in the near future to again have the opportunity of working with you and of obtaining further successes. Signed N.W. Webber, Lieutenant-Colonel General Staff, 2nd Canadian Division.

[6] See CAB 45 200.

[7] It is with great respect to Elles that we point out these errors, but we are sure of our ground, not only in regard to the matters mentioned here but also others less

relevant to our narrative.

8   See *Military Operations: France and Belgium 1916* (part 2), p. 446. The account is wrong only in saying that the tank 'retired by the way it had come'. In fact it had returned along or alongside the Le Barque road.

9   For this and other illustrations, details and analysis of German reaction to the tanks' appearance, see the author's *The Tanks at Flers* (1995).

10   The field on your right is known locally as Le Champ de l'Explosion, and was the place where a vast quantity of surplus munitions was detonated at the end of the war.

11   IWM photograph 682 in Box 162.

Chapter 8

The Butte de Warlencourt:
28 October

The action around the farm at Eaucourt l'Abbaye and the capture of Le Sars brought British troops within sight, and within close range, of the Butte de Warlencourt, a chalk mound off to the right of the main road leading to Bapaume. This was a prehistoric earthwork whose original purpose was, and still is, shrouded in mystery. The material for its construction was quarried from an area immediately north-west of it, between it and the road, the site now a sizeable depression.

In late 1916 the Butte and the ground around it presented a ghastly picture. Its significance as a platform from which to survey the surrounding ground was fully understood by both sides, the Germans fortifying it with abundant machine guns and the British pounding it with all types of artillery. The scene was one of utter devastation.

On 12 October III Corps called for 9th Division to capture first the German defences at the Tail, the Pimple and Snag Trench, then the Butte itself. Alas, the attack made little progress – unsurprisingly, given the conditions and the enemy's dominating position. Nonetheless, by late October the British had forced their way towards it over ground now churned into a muddy, glutinous morass. Casualties were heavy, for any progress eastwards from Le Sars was perforce made under the eyes of the defenders, across a shallow valley. In consequence, any further advance was blocked.

However, the need to capture the Butte and put an end to the threat which it posed to the British was apparent to all. Preparations were made for another attack on 28 October by 50th Division, now supported by two tanks – one male, the other female – details being given in the division's GX2868/1 of 25 October. This called for the male machine to move during the night of 27th/28th to a position about M23a 9.4, the crossroads lying some 180m north-east of the farm at Eaucourt. It was then to move at Zero in the direction of

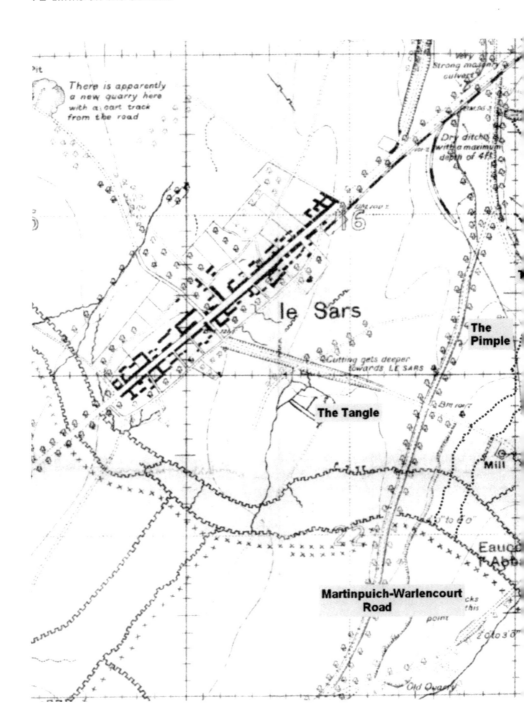

There is apparently a new quarry here with a cart track from the road

Very Strong masonry culvert

Dry ditch with a maximum depth of 4ft

le Sars

The Pimple

Cutting gets deeper towards LE SARS

The Tangle

Mill

Eau

Martinpuich-Warlencourt Road

Old Quarry

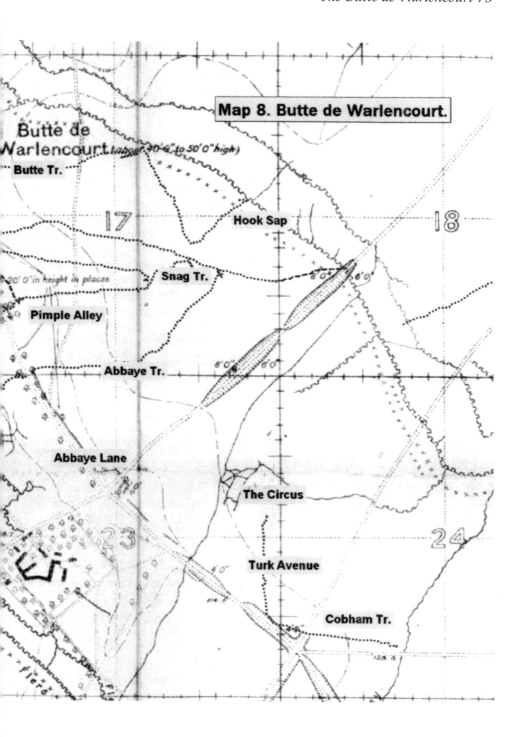

Map 8. Butte de Warlencourt.

Hook Trench (or Hook Sap, M17d 5.8) and assist the infantry to take this if they had not been able to do so before the tank arrived. It was then to proceed to the final objective in Gird Trench and Gird Support (specified as being about M18a 0.0) and later, after seeing the infantry firmly settled in, to return to its starting point at the crossroads.

The female was to move to M17c 2.6 during the night, this being a point on the road leading from the same crossroads referred to above, round the west side of the Butte. Like its consort, this tank was to start at Zero and no doubt to stay on the road for 350–450m, for it was then to advance between the Butte and the Quarry. Should the infantry fail to reach the Butte before the arrival of the tank, they were to make another effort in conjunction with it. Whether or not they were successful, the tank was to continue to move forward and do all in its power to protect the right flank of 15th Division, advancing on the left of the main road, from enfilade fire directed from the Butte. 'It will then remain out on the Objective north of the Butte until our infantry have secured the Objective, when it will return to its starting point.'

In the event, this attack did not take place on the 28th, owing to the appalling weather. And when it did, on 5 November, the tanks took no part, for it was clear that they could make no progress through the mud. Instead, the infantry had to attempt the task on their own. With incredible courage, men of the Durham Light Infantry floundered forward, seized the Butte in the face of the fiercest opposition and held the Quarry throughout the day, only to be repulsed by determined German counter-attacks at midnight. The Germans' positions here then remained in place until their withdrawal to the Hindenburg Line in March 1917.

We do not know the names of the commanders selected for the abandoned tank action nor do we know the numbers of their tanks. In parentheses, however, it seems strange that the machine selected to go closest to the Butte was a female, whose Vickers would have been less effective than the male's 6-pdrs in destroying the machine-gun emplacements dug deep into the slopes above.

Field Guide
IGN Map 2407E
The start point is the crossroads north-east of Eaucourt l'Abbaye at spot height 108 on the modern IGN map. From here drive or walk along the rough track leading north. The 1916 reference M17c 2.6 is half-way between spot heights 103 and 101. From here you can carry on to the end of the road and turn right, past the Quarry, to visit the Butte above you. The Objective of the male tank, had it gone into action, was at M18a 0.0 on Gird Trench but well to the east of the Butte, about the second 'e' of La Madeleine on the IGN map.

Tank Operations:
RESERVE ARMY
(General Sir Hubert Gough)

re-named on 30 October 1916
FIFTH ARMY

North-west of the Albert–Bapaume road
September–November 1916

Chapter 9

Thiepval Ridge:
26 September

Thiepval village and the ridge which it guarded had been important targets for the British X Corps on 1 July. The ridge ran from Thiepval almost to Courcelette, its dominating position over the surrounding ground giving the Germans an enormous advantage over the attacking force; and this, together with the resolute defence and well-sited trench works which the British encountered – especially in the village and the formidable Schwaben Redoubt – meant that, despite dogged courage, the attackers were unable to advance far. The 36th (Ulster) Division, fighting its way across an area lying north-west and north of the village, made the deepest penetration but was unable to hold for more than a day the ground which it had won.

The assault by 32nd Division on the village itself and the ground to its south achieved little and in the following weeks the British were able only to nibble away at the German positions there. Nearby, some progress was made – albeit at great cost – astride the main Albert–Bapaume highway. La Boisselle and Ovillers fell in July, as did Pozières in August and Courcelette on 15 September, when the tanks made their debut in war, but the ridge linking Thiepval and Courcelette remained in German hands.

Sir Douglas Haig was determined to capture this ground as soon as his resources permitted. The tanks' performance on the 15th, however modest in the eyes of some, had convinced him of their potential usefulness, and he considered that an advance now across the ridge, again with their assistance, would enable him to bring greater pressure to bear on the Germans holding out north of the Ancre.

South of the river his plan involved two separate corps of Gough's Reserve Army. The Canadian Corps was to advance north and north-east of Courcelette while the British II Corps, its flank protected by the Canadians, was to capture Thiepval, then go on to take Schwaben, Zollern and Stuff

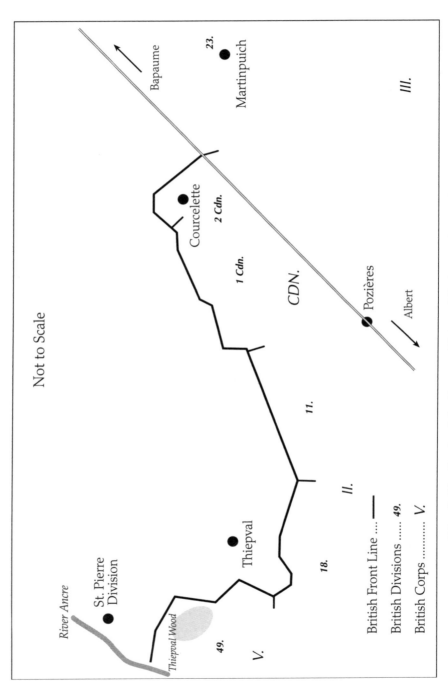

Not to Scale

River Ancre

St. Pierre
Division

Thiepval Wood

Thiepval

49.

V.

18.

II.

11.

CDN.

1 Cdn.

2 Cdn.

Courcelette

Pozières

Albert

Bapaume

Martinpuich

23.

III.

British Front Line ....⎯
British Divisions ...... *49.*
British Corps .... *V.*

Map 9. The Battle of the Somme: Thiepval Ridge, 26 September 1916.

Redoubts on the ridge and advance down into the Ancre valley. Following Haig's discussions with Rawlinson on 20 September, a GHQ instruction of the same day directed that as many tanks as Fourth Army could spare from south of the Albert–Bapaume road should be transferred at once to the Reserve Army north of it, to reach the latter by midday on the 22nd at the latest, in readiness for an attack to begin on the 23rd if the weather held, otherwise as soon as possible thereafter.

With the Canadian Corps: 1st and 2nd Canadian Divisions

Of the eight machines transferred from Fourth Army, six were allotted to II Corps and two to the Canadian Corps, the latter being Lieutenant F.A. Robinson in D22 (tank no. 745) and Second Lieutenant E.C.K. Colle in D25 (no. 511). Both were D Company tanks and both had been in action on the 15th, when Colle's efforts in aiding 50th Division had earned him an MC 'for conspicuous gallantry in action. He fought his tank with great gallantry, reaching the Third Objective. Later, on several occasions he went to the assistance of the infantry, and finally brought his tank safely out of action.'

Robinson had been with 47th Division on the 15th in High Wood. He had achieved a sort of distinction in the battle by veering away from his allotted path in the wood, ditching in a nearby British-held trench outside it and spraying the occupants with machine-gun fire. For this he earned a 'roasting' from the infantry commanding officer but also, surprisingly, an MC as well. Now, eleven days later, he was again in command of D22, dug out from the trench near High Wood with apparently little damage, and ready for this new operation in support of the Canadians' 2nd Division attack immediately north-east of Courcelette and that of their 1st Division to the north and north-west.

In doing this Robinson was, as we say, to be accompanied by Colle in D25, but this machine became ditched when coming up through Pozières and played no part in the day's action. It was dug out on 28 September and returned to the Loop.

D Company's War Diary says Robinson's orders – and those of Colle had he been there – were 'to proceed from Albert to Courcelette and cruise round village while infantry consolidated'. This, of course, was hardly the sort of detailed instruction which a tank commander had the right to expect, but it was evidently amended well before Robinson went into action. The failure of the Northumberland Fusiliers to follow Enoch's advance against Twenty-Sixth Avenue the day before meant that the Germans there still threatened the Canadians' advance northwards twenty-four hours later.

Robinson was therefore now ordered to reach M25b 2.4 in the centre of Courcelette before daybreak, then proceed to a start-point at M25b 6½.1 (more correctly expressed as M25b 65.10), which was a point 275m down the road

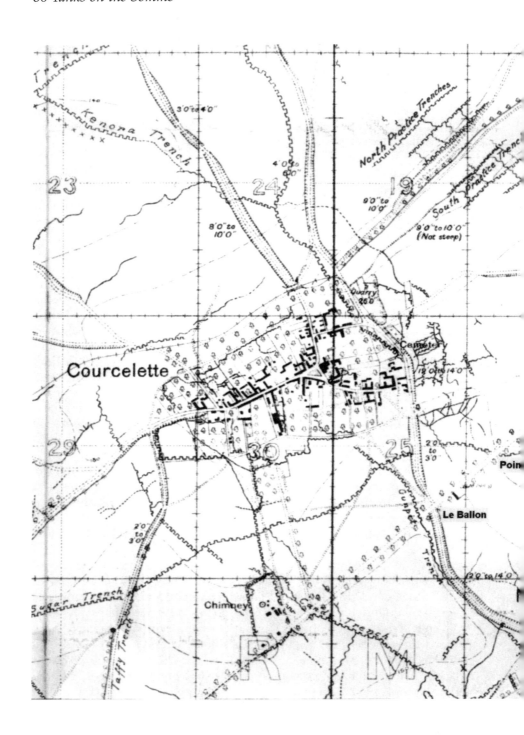

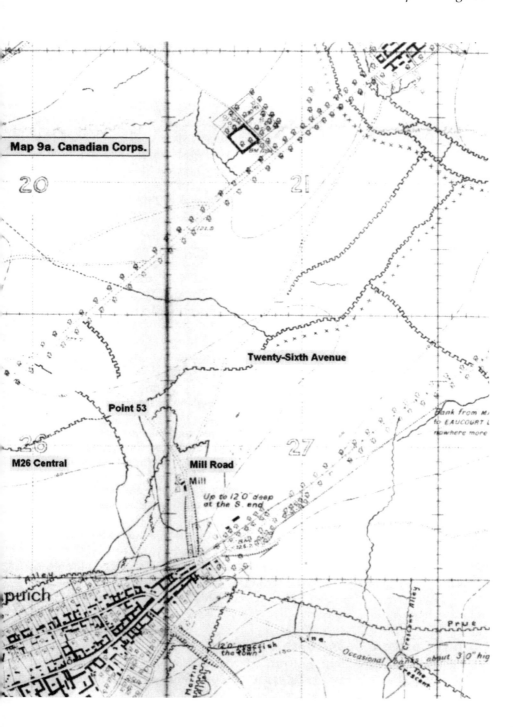

Map 9a. Canadian Corps.

20

21

Twenty-Sixth Avenue

Point 53

Bank from M
to EAUCOURT L
nowhere more

26

27

M26 Central

Mill Road

Mill

Up to 12'0" deep
at the S. end

Alley

pnch

Prue

the town

Occasional banks about 3'0" hig

The Crescent

leading to the north-east corner of Courcelette from Le Ballon crossroads on the main highway. From here he was to move eastwards along the rear of Twenty-Sixth Avenue and clear it of the enemy as far as the main road. From there he was to turn due north, attacking any Germans left in the trenches near the village, then carry on via South and North Practice Trenches (formerly German training grounds either side of Dyke Road), all the while helping the Canadian infantry to establish posts from which they could bring enfilade machine-gun fire to bear on German-held trenches. Having done this, he was to continue round in a wide arc and return to his base via the western outskirts of the village.

But his immediate task was to help the Canadians' 28th Battalion to eject the Germans from Twenty-Sixth Avenue. The War Diary of D Company says that he 'carried out all orders till tank was hit by H.E. and blown up on east side of Courcelette', but this was not strictly true. He was, of course, never able to 'cruise round the village' and his revised role was of brief duration. He set out on his mission at 11.54 a.m. and advanced along the north side of the German trench as far as M26a 1.½ (M26a 10.05), apparently covering the 225m in just three minutes, which would indicate a speed of 2.8 mph – rather fast, one might think, for a Mark I travelling over ground that was almost certainly cratered. As soon as he appeared, the enemy withdrew in order to escape the barrage which their artillery promptly laid down, aimed at stopping the tank's further progress. In this it succeeded, for at 12.05 p.m. Robinson turned back to the Canadian lines at M25b 8.1. The shelling, however, had followed him and at 12.20 p.m. he and his men abandoned the tank. Two members of the crew were wounded.

The men of 28th Battalion, forming the extreme right of the divisional front, were understandably disappointed at losing what had promised to be a valuable aid to their advance over open ground. They therefore cancelled their part of the attack due to begin at 12.35 p.m. The Germans, no doubt guessing what had happened, proceeded to filter back into the area in considerable numbers but, lacking protection, were there mown down by Canadian machine gunners.

At 2.12 p.m. D22 caught fire and its ammunition later exploded. The Canadian Corps War Diary says simply that 'a tank, having reached the front line, was heavily shelled and had to be abandoned'. There are numerous photographs of the wreck, taken later in the war.

It has to be said that neither Robinson nor Colle had been of great value to the Canadians in this engagement.

With II Corps: 11th and 18th Divisions

As we say, two of the eight tanks transferred to Gough's Reserve Army by Rawlinson's Fourth Army, both from D Company, were allotted to the

Looking east along the Vallée Vircholle. The road from Ginchy and the Quadrilateral, both off to the right, drops down to A then crosses the valley before rising at B en route to Morval. The Tortillard (the 'Twister') narrow-gauge railway at C snakes its way through the fields and through cuttings now shrouded in trees on its way to Combles in the distance. The British cleared the long finger of Bouleux Wood down to its northern end here at D but were held up by German machine guns in the copse at E. These were finally destroyed by the infantry before Bates arrived on the scene, his tank apparently becoming ditched in the field at F.

Aerial view towards Morval from above the point where the A1 and A2 motorways merge, across the line of the TGV high-speed railway. Mutton Trench lay to the left (west) of the now much foreshortened track which in 1916 led to Haie Wood, today half-buried under the roadway, then towards Fregicourt out of sight in the rear. Dashwood's tank came to grief at X when leaving the main road out of the village in order to attack Mutton Trench from behind. The road at A leads from and to Lille, those at B and C come from and to Cambrai.

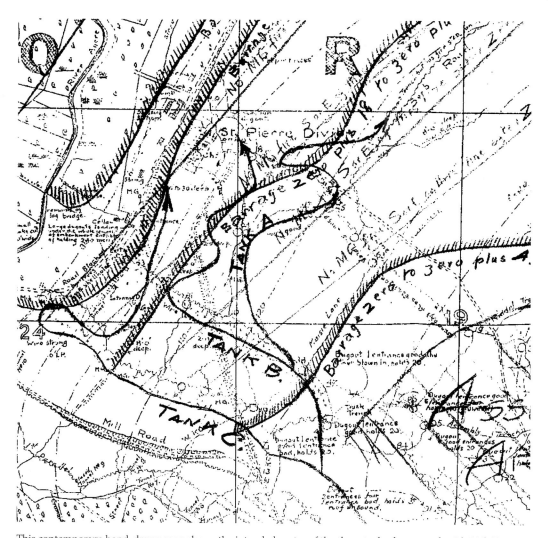

This contemporary, hand-drawn map shows the intended routes of the three tanks due to work with 39th Division on 13 November. The infantry were to set out from their assembly area north and west of the Schwaben Redoubt, shown near the lower corner, and follow the artillery barrage. The successive lines of the standing barrages ("Barrage Zero to Zero plus 4'; Barrage Zero plus 18' to Zero plus 22', etc.") are indicated by hatching, whilst the thin lines indicate the limits of machine-gun fire ("No machine-gun fire S or E of this line after Zero plus 4' etc."). Meanwhile the tanks were to emerge from their base south of Thiepval Wood and later to take their separate ways north of it, as shown here. In the event only one of them (A13, tank C for this operation) was able to proceed.

The ground in front of Gueudecourt, seen from the south-west. A marks the place where Storey began his attack on Gird Trench. The letters B, B, B trace the first part of this long defence line and therefore his route up to the point where it crossed over Watling Street, the Chemin des Guilmonniers. The pond is at C, where a road branches off, up towards Point 91 (beyond the right of the picture).

Looking north over Martinpuich towards the Albert–Bapaume road which runs from left to right far in the distance. Twenty-Sixth Avenue, which formed the German front line, lay on the near (south) side of the road, while the British line was nearer the village. The start point originally specified for Enoch was M26d 0.3, just out of the picture on the left, but in the absence of Colle he may have preferred to start from a point further to the right, nearer his target. After approaching the enemy defence line he then circled round anti-clockwise to finish up back in the British line at A.

The farm of Les Marquays, established after the war just outside Thiepval on the road to Pozières. The tank supporting 53rd Brigade (*Cognac*'s unspecified companion) was ditched in the Schwaben Graben at A. Another tank, also unspecified, was ditched at B. The Schwaben Redoubt extended from C to C, from the fields just beyond the triangular civil cemetery (hidden in the the trees) across to the right towards the post-war Grande Ferme or L'Ecamperche.

D18, left on the battlefield at Martinpuich and drawn in his notebook by Captain E. Shirley-Jones of D Company, 1/8th Worcestershire Regiment in December 1916. (Drawing presented to the Tank Museum by Brigadier N.W. Duncan in 1948.)

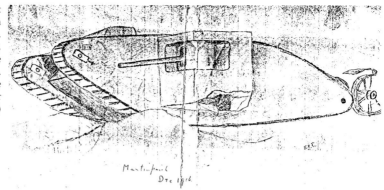

The Thiepval area seen from the east. The two tanks of the 'Western Couple' started out from near the copse at A. Inglis in *Crème de Menthe* finished up hanging part of the way over the road embankment at B, to the right of the farm where the Chateau once stood. His companion came to a halt in what is now the *allée* between the trees at C. Traces of the old trench works are still visible. See for instance the former German front line just beyond the farm.

We believe that the tank in the foreground of this photograph of the road leading north from Flers is Storey's, recovered after its spectacular attack on the Gird Line and the village of Gueudecourt on 26 September, then left here after it had suffered a broken track. The machine is, of course, a male, whereas reports say that Storey's was a female, 516, but this was the tank in which Storey set out on 15 September, only to ditch shortly after he started. Ten days later he was in his 'new' D4, a quite different machine, although bearing the same company designation.

These two tanks beside the Albert–Bapaume road, being demolished by German prisoners-of-war, are undoubtedly those of Lieutenants Phillips and Hopkins, put out of action by German shellfire on 23 October. They are both female machines. The building in the distance is almost certainly the remains of the Courcelette Sugar Factory, the capture of which by the 2nd Canadian Division on 15 September was aided by two tanks of C Company. If this identification is correct, the wrecked tanks are lying almost exactly where today the Tank memorial stands on the highest point of the Pozières Ridge.

Ariadne, which despite its name is evidently a male. Only just visible in each lower corner is a marker showing Le Sars on the left and Martinpuich on the right, coordinates which would place the wreck somewhere north of the tree-lined Dyke Road running eastward from Courcelette. Allowing for a degree of licence and even error on Wheeler's part (not unknown in his other writings), *Ariadne* must be the tank that he claims he and his companion inspected during the fighting which raged around this part of the battlefield.

Serre Road No. 2 Cemetery, where over 7,000 British and Commonwealth soldiers lie buried, occupies what in 1916 was no-man's-land between the German Heidenkopf, roughly at the far corner of the cemetery, and the British lines to the right of the photograph.

The point where Bruce or Telford came to grief, just beyond the German front line in front of Beaumont Hamel.

Canadian Corps (see above) and six to II Corps. It is, of course, true that Gough already had a few C Company tanks at his disposal, including the three machines of its No. 1 Section surviving from their action in support of the Canadians between Pozières and Courcelette on the 15th.[1] There had originally been six machines in that section, all named after French drinks. Of these, *Champagne* (C1), *Chartreuse* (C3) and *Chablis* (C4) were still lying on the battlefield, out of action, but three had returned: *Cognac* (C2), *Crème de Menthe* (C5) and *Cordon Rouge* (C6). These were almost certainly now back in the same former quarry, shown as Old Chalk Pit on British trench maps, that had served them as shelter only a few days before, tucked in against the rising ground known as Le Chemin Blanc, east of Aveluy and the River Ancre. They were undoubtedly joined there by others, including some of the tanks sent across from Fourth Army, but the identity of these latter is not always clear.

11th Division

In the sector assigned to 11th Division, the First Objective set for the infantry extended from a point on Zollern Trench East at R28a 3.6 via the gravel pit at R27c 5.4 and the tree at R32b 7.9 to a point along Schwaben Trench at R26c 9.3. The Second extended from a point on Hessian Trench at R22c 1.9 via the junction of Baden Street and Zollern Trench West at R27a 5.9 and along to join up with 18th Division at R26b 0.2. The Third Objective extended from R22c 1.9 (acting as a pivot), along the northern edge of Stuff Redoubt, then along Hessian Trench to the junction of this with Midway Line.

The Corps Commander, Lieutenant-General C.W. Jacob, had decided that only two of his six tanks should operate with 11th Division, and these were allotted to its 34th Brigade on the right of the divisional front. Both machines were said to have started from a point west of Pozières, this of course being no more than a temporary post closer to their sector of the front line than the main base at the Chalk Pit.

The orders given to them were to follow up the attacking infantry but not to precede them, except at the outset, when they were to arrive at Mouquet Farm at Zero, just as the main body of infantry was leaving the jumping-off trenches some distance in the rear. There was, however, some confusion on this point, divisional orders laying it down that the tanks were to stay in their 'positions of concealment' in the rear until Zero, which would naturally have delayed their entry onto the battlefield itself. Just how the matter was resolved on this particular day is not made evident in the documents, but subsequent instructions from II Corps would have called for greater clarity on the issue.

At Zero, 12.35 p.m., the infantry surged forward under the artillery barrage and at first their attack went well. They moved swiftly past Mouquet Farm, although in their eagerness to press ahead they failed to clear out its occupants. Zollern Trench West was taken without much difficulty by about

1.20 p.m., and many prisoners were taken, but beyond this point the advance was checked by machine-gun fire from Bulgar Trench and from points to its north. This was precisely the sort of circumstance that called for tank support, but the *Official History* tells us that both machines had become ditched even before reaching Mouquet Farm. Trench maps, on the other hand, show that one at least reached within a few yards of it, where doubtless it became stuck in one of the myriad shell holes among and around the German defence-works there. The crew got out and supported the infantry attack on the farm, as the War Diary of 34th Brigade tells us:

> At 4.30 p.m. the occupants of the farm were causing many casualties, so Lieutenant Dancer, 3rd Dorsets, the officer of tank No. 542 and its crew and Lieutenant Kohnstamm and six men of 11th Manchesters and a sergeant and six men of the 6th East Yorkshire Pioneers lined the top of a mound on the building and placed two machine guns from the tanks to cover the western and northern entrances to the farm, while two bombing parties of the 11th Manchesters threw bombs down the entrances to the farm with no visible result. At 5.30 p.m. Lieutenant Low of 11th Manchesters threw bombs down the entrances and shortly afterwards the occupants came out – one officer and fifty-five other ranks . . . The actual taking of the farm cannot be claimed by any one unit, as 6th East Yorkshires, 11th Manchesters, 5th Dorsets and No. 542 tank were all represented.[2]

Alas, we do not know the identity of tank 542's commander, nor its name, nor is there any reference that we have seen to the precise point where its companion machine was ditched.

18th Division

Two tanks having been allocated by II Corps to 11th Division, the remaining four were given to 18th Division, which was thought to have the harder task, being up against more formidable defences in and around the village.

Two of the four, known within the division as the Eastern Couple, were to support the division's 53rd Brigade by advancing up Nab Valley (later called Blighty Valley) to reach the Pozières–Thiepval road at R26c 3.4 in order to clear the enemy from the eastern portion of the village. Later, they were to help in the attack on the Schwaben Redoubt.

We know that one of these machines was *Cognac*, no. 522, company designation C2. It had gone into action on the left flank of the Canadians at Courcelette on 15 September, and its commander on that occasion, Lieutenant F.W. Bluemel,[3] was in command of it again today. Gunner Victor Archard, manning one of its Vickers machine guns, has left us an account – not always entirely clear – of its progress once it had left the Chalk Pit at 2 p.m. on the

25th. With some of the crew riding on the roof, enjoying the sunshine, it first travelled north to a nearby crossroads (Crucifix Corner on the map), then headed along the east side of Authuille Wood. Bluemel's first task was to reach an intermediate spot by a quarry at X7a 3.4, said to be near a bend in the road, where he and his crew had a meal before setting out again after dark. Archard and some others went ahead on foot to reconnoitre the route but found progress made difficult and hazardous by quantities of barbed wire and numerous deserted trenches. They eventually found their start point, a quarry near The Nab,[4] one of the most exposed positions on what had been the British front line when the battle opened on 1 July. Here they covered *Cognac* with camouflaged tarpaulins before settling down for a few hours' rest, interrupted only by occasional German shelling and the need to take turns at guard duty.

At 8.30 a.m. on the 26th they and their companions in the second tank breakfasted on bully and biscuits, then spent time cleaning their guns, ready for action. Setting out at Zero, 12.35 p.m., their subsequent progress was reported to Gough's headquarters by the officer commanding the RFC, Major-General H.M. Trenchard, who said both tanks had been seen, 'one behind the other, coming up from R32a'. However, according to the *Official History*, one of them had broken down almost immediately on starting, while Archard himself says that when C2 was negotiating a shell hole a shell exploded in its path and made further advance impossible. The tank bellied, its track unable to get a grip on the soft earth, and it had to be dug out and returned to base in the Chalk Pit at Le Chemin Blanc the following morning.

The other machine was temporarily defeated by an immense crater near the German front line in Joseph Trench but eventually managed to extricate itself and to advance up the valley to the Pozières–Thiepval road, where it soon found itself in dire trouble. It became firmly stuck at R26c 5.4 in Schwaben Trench which lined the road and is said to have received two or three hits from 5.9-inch (150mm) guns which set it on fire.

As for the infantry units in 53rd Brigade, these had led with 8th Suffolk and 10th Essex. Following behind an excellent creeping barrage, they made rapid progress at first through the eastern half of Thiepval, soon meeting up beyond the village with 11th Division on the right and with 54th Brigade on the left. Thereafter progress became slower as the attacking force became exposed to persistent fire from defences further back and from Germans holding out in the north of the village. A partial withdrawal was ordered.

The commander of 18th Division, Major-General Maxse, had chosen his 54th Brigade to lead the attack in the area of Thiepval Chateau and the western half of the village, and to do so on a frontage of just one of its battalions, the 12th Middlesex. Support was to be provided by two companies of 11th Royal Fusiliers, one acting on the left flank to clear out the innumerable enemy dug-outs along the Germans' original front line of 1 July, now to be

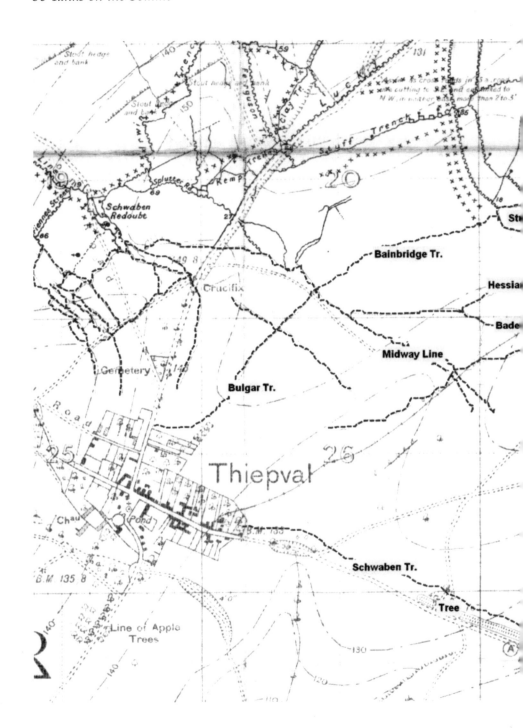

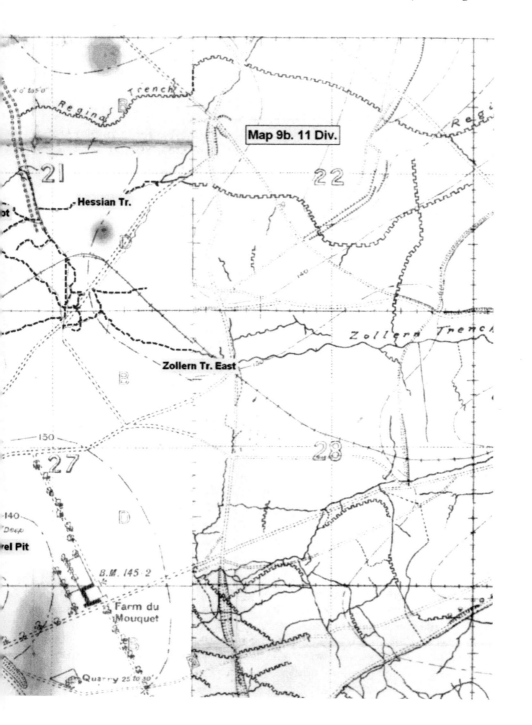

attacked in enfilade, and the other behind the Middlesex as moppers-up. Behind them came the two remaining companies, ordered either to support the leading infantry or to assist in the work of clearing out the enemy from cellars and other shelters.

Behind the Middlesex and Fusiliers came the 6th Northamptonshires in support, while the 7th Bedfordshires were held in reserve.

The Brigade was allocated the remaining two (the Western Couple) of the division's four tanks, and it was decided that these should start from Caterpillar Dump near the small Caterpillar Copse at Q30d 3.0, south of Thiepval Wood. Their immediate target was to be the Chateau, after capturing which they were to join the two tanks working with 53rd Brigade and attack the southern face of the Schwaben Redoubt. During the morning, but well before Zero, the entire crew of each tank was to examine the ground over which their advance was to take place and become acquainted with any landmarks available. A similar instruction had been given to the Eastern Couple, but we do not have details of how this reconnaissance in either case was to be carried out.

As one of the tanks, C5 *Crème de Menthe*, commanded by Captain A.M. Inglis, moved up and across the former no-man's-land of 1 July, it encountered an enemy machine gun, reportedly at R25c 7.7, which was giving great trouble to the men of 11th Royal Fusiliers trying to advance along the old German front line. This coordinate is well within no-man's-land, indeed about half-way across it, and if correct shows great daring on the part of the German crew, who had sited their gun well forward in order to inflict maximum damage on the Fusiliers moving behind them. They were eventually silenced by the tank as it passed on its way to the Chateau. For a while it seemed as if the Germans were concentrating all their artillery fire and much of their machine-gun fire on this lone machine rather than on the infantry, for the latter were reported at one stage to be advancing steadily forward without much trouble. This state of affairs did not, however, last for long. Many casualties among the Middlesex and Fusiliers were now caused by machine guns firing from the area of the Chateau ruins, but the War Diary of 54th Brigade says that the 'opportune' arrival of the tank effectively silenced these:

> It seems doubtful, if the Chateau defence had not been dealt with by the tank, whether the attack would have progressed beyond that line. As it was, the assaulting companies of the 12th Middlesex passed it right and left. Unfortunately this tank, after passing the Chateau, was ditched about 100 yards north of it and, resting at a very steep angle, was unable to use any of its armament...A strong-point was made around the stranded tank at R25d 3.8. This consisted of machine guns taken out of the tank and about twenty additional men.[5]

This map reference is reflected with great accuracy on later trench maps, where a small circle headed 'derelict tank' appears. This, the brigade's First Objective, lay along part of the sunken road which ran from south-east to north-west through Thiepval, and the cartographer – no doubt basing himself on a survey taken after the battle – has evidently tried to show that the tank was on, or indeed partly over, the edge of the embankment and therefore at the 'steep angle' which the diarist mentions. Its identity as *Creme de Menthe* is confirmed by reports later on when, still lying abandoned on the battlefield, it served as a shelter for an infantry signals section.[6]

There are other coordinates given for the position of this tank, for instance R25d 5.9, which is 90m up the road leading to Grandcourt, where it was said to be under heavy shell-fire at 1.15 p.m. Less improbably, another is shown on 18th Division's own map as being not on the embankment but on flat ground a few yards short of it at R25d 3.7.

Yet another, timed at 6.35 p.m., was reported by an RFC observer, Lieutenant E. O'Hanlon of 4 Squadron, who said that, 'The tank at R25d 3.6 is coming to life again.' We cannot explain this, as the position indicated is right up against the north wall of the Chateau, 100m or so from the embankment. As no other mention is made of this move, we imagine the tank's motion was very brief and its position incorrectly reported.

It is, of course, difficult to plot the exact path of the tanks, partly because in the heat of battle errors were often made when noting the coordinates. Also, the War Diaries do not always make it clear whether the timing given was that when the event occurred, when it was recorded by the observer, when it was sent to base, or when it was received there. In O'Hanlon's case we have his pencilled note, evidently dropped from his aircraft to troops on the ground, saying explicitly 6.35 p.m., but mistakes can happen. Nonetheless, for the reasons stated we think the coordinate given by 54th Brigade in the passage quoted above and recorded on the trench map is likely to be accurate.

We assume that the commander of this tank was the same officer as on the 15th, Captain Arthur Maculloch Inglis, who distinguished himself on that earlier occasion by his action at the Sugar Factory at Courcelette, for which he was awarded the DSO.

The report by 54th Brigade says that the second tank starting from Caterpillar Copse arrived too late to be of any value and was ditched 'between R25c 8.1 and R25d 5.9'. Alas, these map references are virtually meaningless for they lie at least 450m apart. The first bears no relation to references given in other reports and the second is merely a repeat of the erroneous reference quoted above.

There is, indeed, a 'derelict tank' marked on later trench maps at R25d 03.17, but the cartographer who showed its location – correctly, we believe – cannot have been helped by the rather woolly description given in this case by

54th Brigade. He must instead have surveyed its position after the battle. The failure of this machine to arrive in time for the early fighting, and its inability to participate in the fighting thereafter, must have been a severe blow to the attacking British troops. Its identity is not revealed in the War Diaries but the history of 18th Division, published after the war, says it was *Cordon Bleu*, obviously an error for *Cordon Rouge*, tank C6, commanded with great success by Second Lieutenant J. Allan, in conjunction with Inglis, at Courcelette on the 15th. We think it most likely that he was again in command of the tank on this later occasion, paired with Inglis in *Crème de Menthe* as part of a winning team. Whether their continued presence and that of the other tanks in this sector would have enabled the British to capture Schwaben Redoubt on this day, as called for by Gough, is not something that we can pronounce on with assurance, but without them the infantry were unable finally and completely to subdue the strong-point until they drove out its occupants on 14 October.

Field Guide

IGN Maps 2407O, 2407E & 2408O

The quarry which served as a base for the tanks operating in this sector was the same as the one used by those attached to the 2nd Canadian Division on 15 September. It is shown as Old Chalk Pit on later trench maps. Some doubt about this identification was expressed in our earlier book *The Tanks at Flers*, prompted by a rather puzzling description in the records, but the author is now convinced that it was sited here.[7] To reach it, take the narrow Chemin d'Authuille in Albert which turns north off the main road leading eventually to Bapaume. Drive along it for 1.75km and on your right you will find the quarry, now no longer used and much greener than it must have been in 1916. The raised walkways of beaten earth that separated each tank 'pen' from its neighbour are still visible on the southern side.

Robinson and Colle would have set out from here for Courcelette, perhaps spending time at some mid-way point. The village, as we have seen, is situated just to the north of the Albert-Bapaume road, where a lone building, Le Ballon, lies close to the Canadian Memorial and gives its name to the nearby crossroads. In 1914 this was the Café National, converted post-war into a private house and renamed, no doubt, after the observation balloons which in 1916 were a frequent feature in the skies above. From here, go down just 270m towards the village. Setting out from here, Robinson entered the field on the north-east side of the road, then kept to the north side of the enemy trench, Twenty-Sixth Avenue, which went on to cross the road to Bapaume 250m from Le Ballon. There is not much here to distinguish his route but he apparently returned almost to his start point before being brought to a halt.

Bluemel's *Cognac* and its unidentified companion, both assigned to 53rd

Brigade of 18th Division, set out for Crucifix Corner, 500m to the north of the Chalk Pit. This is where four roads meet, but where a fifth, at first asphalted but thereafter no more than a track, leads north from a point slightly to the right. *Cognac* must have taken this route, keeping just inside the wood (Authuille Wood to the British but Bois de la Haie on the IGN map) as it then curled round to the right. The quarry at X7a 3.4 where the tanks waited for dusk is not a prominent feature and we wonder if this is an error for X1c 5.1 where a larger quarry is certainly found. A further quarry, which may be the one used by the tanks as their start point at Zero on the 26th, is shown on the trench map at X1b 5.2, very near The Nab of 1 July. It lay immediately on the north side of the Ovillers–Authuille road where this reaches its lowest point half-way between the two villages. Although the area is now partly sheltered from view by trees, there is little sign of a quarry here today. A possible alternative candidate is a fairly large quarry about 80m inside the wood on the *south* side of the road but identification cannot be certain.

You may choose to continue this walk beyond the road and up the Valleé Marceau to the point where this divides. Take the left-hand branch – part of 'Thiepval Valley' on British trench maps – and note as you do that on 26 September 1916 the German front line in Joseph Trench lay at 90 degrees across the valley at a point 300m short of the Pozières–Thiepval road. This area, covered by map square R32a, is where General Trenchard claimed his RFC observers had seen both tanks advancing whereas, of course, Archard said his tank, *Cognac*, had broken down earlier on. One or the other must have been wrong. There are indeed two wrecked tanks shown on the main road here, the one on the left, positioned on the opposite northern embankment, being, we believe, *Cognac*'s companion, shown astride Schwaben Trench. The identity of the one on the southern embankment is unknown.

Turning to the tanks with 54th Brigade, *Crème de Menthe* (C5, 721) commanded by Captain Inglis, together with Second Lieutenant Allan in *Cordon Rouge* (C6, 504), would have wound their way northwards from the Old Chalk Pit, passed Crucifix Corner, then waited for nightfall at W11b 5.0, by the bend in the road just short of the entrance to Blighty Valley Cemetery. Later, in darkness, they passed through the village of Authuille, then after 150m branched left along a narrow road now serving holiday homes and camping sites by the river but leading on towards the Bois d'Authuille (spelt Bois d'Hauthuille on later editions of the IGN map, but logically called Thiepval Wood by the British). Before the wood itself is reached, Caterpillar Copse will be seen close up to its side, but separated from it by the Vallée St. Furcy. Caterpillar Dump at Q30d 3.0 was evidently sited half-way up the right-hand edge of the copse.

To follow the later course of the battle, return to the main road and turn back sharp left, up the hill towards Thiepval village. When you reach the

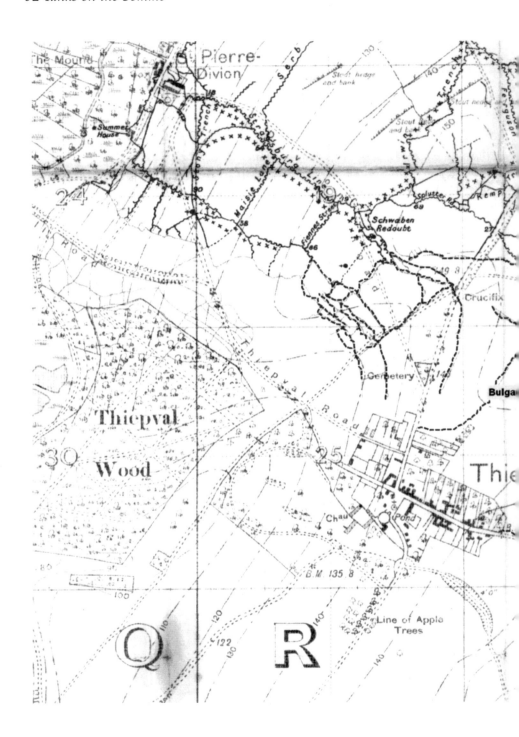

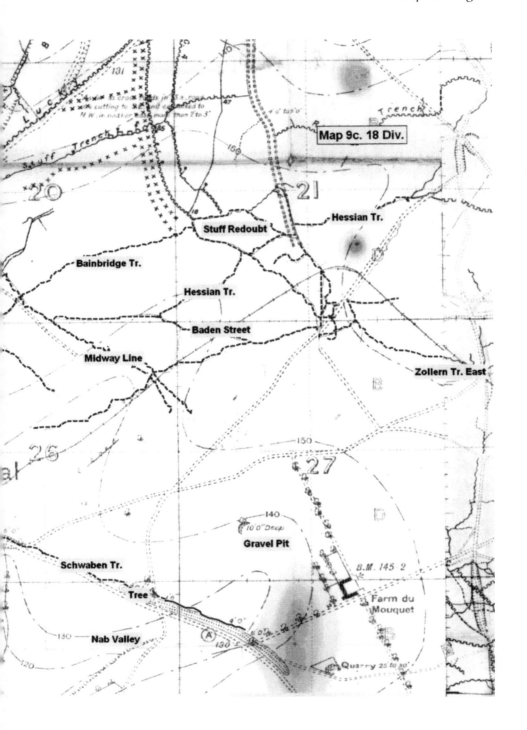

Map 9c. 18 Div.

Hessian Tr.

Stuff Redoubt

Bainbridge Tr.

Hessian Tr.

Baden Street

Midway Line

Zollern Tr. East

Gravel Pit

Schwaben Tr.

Tree

B.M. 145 2

Farm du Mouquet

Nab Valley

Quarry 25 to 30'

obelisk commemorating the 18th Division you will see, on your right, a broad cleared space leading up to the massive Thiepval Memorial. In this space, about 40m or so from the road, and one third in from the wooded area on the right, is where *Cordon Rouge, Crème de Menthe*'s tardy companion, came to a halt.

Now look over the ground on the opposite side of the road here and you will see a field boundary running north-west down to Thiepval Wood. In fact it is also the boundary between the communes of Thiepval and Authuille. It was almost half-way down this – well out into no-man's-land – that the German machine-gun post was sited that Inglis destroyed on his way to the Chateau.

The Chateau itself lay where the present farm buildings are. If, as we believe to be the case, Inglis's tank came to rest hanging part way over the road at R25d 3.8, you can see the place by going up to the crossroads then turning left (north-west) for just 100m.

Turning back in the direction of Pozières, and at a distance of 500m from the crossroads, you will see on the left a cluster of farm buildings, Les Marquays, constructed after the war. We have now, of course, come full circle, for the 'derelict tanks' marked on the map are those discussed above, the first of them, on the left, being *Cognac*'s companion supporting 53rd Brigade.

To reach Mouquet Farm continue towards Pozières for another 900m then turn left up the track. One casualty of the battle – presumably 542 – was lost here but its precise position is obscure. It lay where the post-war farm now sits. The farm's original site on the other side of the track was rendered unsuitable for re-building in the early 1920s because of shell holes, dug-outs, collapsed cellars and, no doubt, unexploded ordnance. The tank's position on the map suggests that the *Official History* could have been just a little ungenerous in saying that neither of the two tanks from Pozières reached Mouquet Farm. This one, at least, got to within 30m of it and its commander and crew evidently assisted in its capture.

As we have said, only six tanks were used by II Corps in this attack but there is evidence on the trench map of unidentified 'derelict tanks' in the vicinity. One is 250m north of Les Marquays, while another lies 200m or so north-west of Stuff Redoubt. We are not aware of any War Diary mention of their presence here, but we assume that they were ditched when proceeding to or from some later engagement further north or east, and then abandoned.

While you are in the Thiepval area why not visit the site of the Schwaben Redoubt? It can be reached by walking up the left-hand side of the triangular civil cemetery just outside Thiepval on the road to Grandcourt. The western face of the redoubt, roughly 100m long, where on 1 July the Germans' greatest firepower was concentrated against the Ulster Division, lay along this track between 500m and 600m from the main road. Later, at the time with which we are concerned in this chapter, the southern face became equally important, but the position of the redoubt on the high ground here gave it a superb field of fire for almost 360 degrees. And down by the Ancre, hidden by the convex slopes north of the redoubt, there were ample German defensive positions along the St Pierre Divion road blocking the path of any British attempt to out-flank the redoubt itself.

---

1   See chapter 11 of *The Tanks at Flers*.

2   Passage quoted from the War Diary of 34th Brigade by Graham Keech in *Pozières*.

3   His family, originally from Germany, owned an engineering firm well-known in Britain for its manufacture of bicycle accessories.

4   A peak in the Lake District of England, an odd choice of name for a low point surrounded by higher ground.

5   In his excellent *The Germans at Thiepval* (see our Introduction), Sheldon quotes a German account which claims to describe an attack on the tanks by troops defending the Chateau area. This is a lurid, imaginative and indeed inventive piece which seeks to highlight the bravery of German soldiers when confronted by the Mark I. Sheldon charitably attributes it to the 'mixed and confused messages' which the German staff received on the subject from front-line troops but, less charitably, we would see it more as a blatant propaganda exercise designed to extract the maximum praise for German valour – an unnecessary task, since that valour was already widely recognised by friend and foe alike. And the drawings of tanks date from a later period, namely the fighting at Bayonet Trench on 18 October. See our own *The Tanks at Flers* and the chapter dealing with that period in this present book.

6   The archives of the Tank Museum at Bovington contain a letter dated 5 March 1974 (reference 04.202) from Captain Bob Morton, formerly Signals Officer with 6th Battalion, Cheshire Regiment. He recalled that when his battalion took over the Thiepval sector on 8 November 1916 he had set up his signals office in a derelict tank which had *H.M.L.S. Crème de Menthe* painted on its side. It had been there since 26 September and was stranded with its nose on a German parados and the rear wheels on the parapet. When his unit moved from Thiepval he left a message inside it saying 'Thanks Tanks: 6th Cheshire Regiment Signals'. See Stedman's *Thiepval*.

7   See chapter 11 of *The Tanks at Flers*, end-note 17 on p. 136. The author and his good friend Jean Verdel debated this question at some length in 2002.

Chapter 10

The Ancre Heights:
October and November

Although they had been forced out of Thiepval village in the fighting of 26 and 27 September, the Germans remained in possession of both the nearby Schwaben Redoubt and the more distant Stuff Redoubt. The men of Lieutenant-General Jacob's II Corps were therefore still faced with the task of seizing these and other major defence lines situated to the north and east before they could finally clear the ground leading down to the Ancre.

We saw in the previous chapter that, as part of its own attempt to clear the high ground between it and Thiepval, the Canadian Corps on the right had mounted an attack east of Courcelette in defence of its flank, where 2nd Canadian Division was to be supported by two tanks. Of these, Colle's D25 was ditched before the attack began, while Robinson's D22 was destroyed after returning from a brief foray into German-held ground. It had been intended that, once they had quelled all opposition on the extreme right, both of these tanks should then describe a wide, anti-clockwise arc around Courcelette for the benefit of both 3rd and 1st Canadian Divisions. In the event, despite the tanks' absence, the infantry made substantial progress north-west of the village, albeit at great cost. It gained substantial portions of its First Objective, Zollern Trench, and its Second, Hessian Trench, and now approached the crest from which it hoped to look down on its Third Objective, Regina Trench (Staufen Riegel).

Fierce fighting continued throughout the next few days, culminating in major attacks on 1 October and again on the 8th. On the far right the Canadians fought their way up as far as the Le Sars Line but then had to relinquish their hold. On their left Stuff Redoubt fell on 9 October, and on the 14th the Germans were finally expelled from the Schwaben. In none of these cases were tanks involved.

Henceforward, however, some on the British side came almost to regard the Germans as less troublesome than the weather and indeed it was already

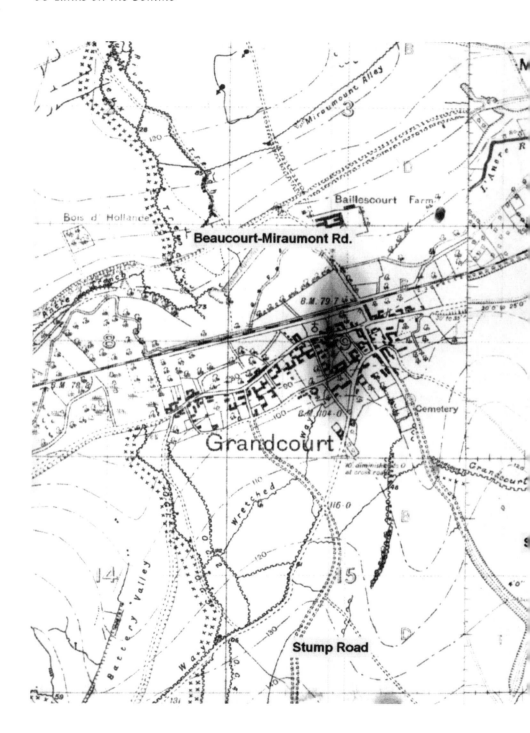

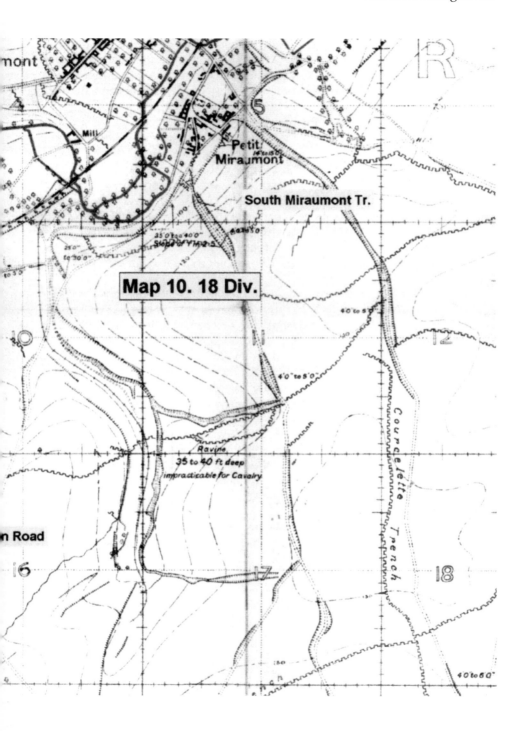

evident that conditions here were likely to frustrate Haig's earlier hopes for a powerful push all along the front. Rain now became heavier and more frequent. Mud lay everywhere and progress through it was slow and therefore dangerous. The mist severely limited artillery and air support. In these conditions the tanks stood little chance of making significant progress.

Partly because of these unfavourable conditions, Haig now formulated entirely new proposals for an advance south and north of the Ancre, these and associated order of battle changes being announced in Reserve Army's Operational Order 32 of 15 October. On the 17th, following several weeks of most arduous duty, the Canadian Corps was relieved and sent to join First Army in the north, taking with it three of its divisions but leaving behind just one, the recently arrived 4th, to be absorbed within II Corps. 18th Division had already sidestepped to the right, nearer to Courcelette, its place nearer Thiepval and Schwaben Redoubt being taken by 39th Division, the intervening space being taken by the 25th Division (relieved on 22 October by the 19th).

Scheduled for 23 October, the plan called for an attack by II Corps across the Ancre and an advance towards Miraumont, but it was to be preceded on the 19th by a preliminary operation designed to secure better 'jumping-off' places for the assaulting troops. A two-day postponement was made necessary by the weather but when it was mounted on the 21st during a brief dry spell this preliminary attack succeeded – without the aid of tanks. However, a two-day postponement had likewise been thought necessary in the main operation, details being given in II Corps' Operational Order 45 of 22 October. This called for 18th, 19th and 39th Divisions on the 25th to capture Pys, Irles, Achiet-le-Petit and Miraumont and also to cross the Ancre to capture the area lying between it and the Miraumont–Beaucourt road. Later in the day the 4th Canadian Division was to extend to the right, seize the Quadrilateral[1] and support III Corps of Fourth Army in its advance on the Butte de Warlencourt. The whole movement was to be mounted in conjunction with an eastward thrust by V Corps north of the Ancre.

To the despair, no doubt, of staff planners in both II and V Corps, that brief spell of reasonable weather was quickly followed by a return of the mist and heavy rain, causing the main operation, already re-scheduled from the 23rd to the 25th, to be repeatedly postponed.

Preparations, however, had to go on, although this time tanks were to be used. At a Corps conference on 23 October, Lieutenant-General Jacob described the manner in which these would be employed:

> Every possible effort will be made to get the tanks into position, and to ensure their carrying out their tasks. Divisional Commanders must not however depend too much on the assistance which will be given to them by the tanks, and all their plans must be prepared on the assumption that

they may have to do without this assistance. Whatever happens, the infantry must not wait for the tanks.

Divisional Commanders are responsible that it is brought to the notice of everyone that we have such a preponderance of artillery that we ought to be able to fight our way through without the assistance of the tanks and, further, that in no circumstances are the attacking troops to wait for the tanks to move but are always to follow close behind the artillery barrage.

Of the fifty-two tanks available for the new operations – the majority now assembled behind the lines at Acheux – twenty tanks were allocated to II Corps and thirty-two to V Corps. A Reserve Army instruction of 18 October had already ruled that four of the tanks allocated to II Corps (six in the case of V Corps) were to be kept in reserve for use against more distant targets should the need arise, but both II Corps and V Corps later commented to Reserve Army that the number of breakdowns that had already occurred among the tank force while getting them into position meant that there would probably be none available for that reserve. Breakdowns, however, were not the only reason for their diminishing numbers, for it was reported that two tanks of A Company, commanded by Second-Lieutenants Phillips and Hopkins, both on loan from the newly arrived B Company, had been hit by German shells on 23 October while 'lying up' on the Albert–Bapaume road.[2]

The principal thrust in this sector was to be delivered by 18th Division, which was to be given ten tanks, all apparently belonging to the Heavy Section's A Company commanded by Major C.M. Tippetts, which had arrived in France just too late to take part in the Battle of Flers-Courcelette. Their orders were spelt out in a divisional instruction G.391 of 23 October. The group was to be headed by Captain P.L. Jackson MC, the commander of A Company's no. 1 Section, comprising four tanks (probably those of Lieutenants Cockrell, Diamond, Dorman and Vardy), but evidently the group now included tanks borrowed from other sections as well. Clearly his task was a demanding one, for it involved an advance of over 2750m just to reach South Miraumont Trench, and even further to reach the village of Petit Miraumont – the way barred by trenches, wire and, more significantly, by deep mud and a shell-torn terrain. The difficulties thus presented caused II Corps to warn Fifth Army HQ (Reserve Army was renamed Fifth Army on 30 October) that unless the ground dried out considerably all the tanks might be confined to the East Miraumont Road, where at least the portion between Courcelette and Regina Trench had been prepared for their passage.

From the last paragraph of these instructions it appears that one of Jackson's tanks was to proceed up the east side of the road in order to assist the 4th Canadian Division, which was to advance alongside the 18th for part of the way. We will return to this subject later.

The First Objective for 18th Division was that stretch of Grandcourt Trench which lay between the East Miraumont Road (Courcelette Trench on Map 10) and Sixteen Road. The Second Objective lay along the Albert–Arras railway line and the Third was Miraumont itself. Beyond this lay the heights of Beauregard, after which the division would turn west and meet up with V Corps' 37th Division advancing from the Redan and from Frankfort and Munich Trenches (see later chapters).

On 18th Division's left, 19th Division was to have four tanks, under Captain Raikes of A Company's no. 4 Section, targeted in the first instance against Grandcourt village. They were all to start out from the same place, R21a 4.7, being a point on the front line in Stuff Trench immediately west of Stump Road, and were numbered, for planning purposes, from 1 to 4.

Tank no. 1 was apparently targeted against the crossroads in the village at R9b 1.1½, and was to reach this by going down the opposite, east side of Stump Road. Since this road is 'sunken' – and deeply so – it is difficult to see how its commander can have carried out his orders without at first reversing a long way to where the steep embankments flattened out sufficiently for him to cross. But as the instruction given to him was the revised version of an earlier order, one would naturally suppose that the divisional staff had had time to reflect on exactly what they were now asking the tank commanders to do.

However, the evidence makes us think that they did not do so. It is true that the other machines had easier tasks to perform: Tank no. 2, for instance, was to aim for the crossroads at R9a 7.0, Tank no. 3 for the crossroads at R9c 1½.6, and Tank no. 4 for the less specific 'west end' of the village. But the instructions went on to say that once Grandcourt had been secured, the two nearest available tanks were to proceed via the railway bridge at R8c Central to the north of the river and attack Baillescourt Farm, capturing en route the trenches to the south of Bois d'Hollande. Since the 'bridge' in question is clearly shown on the map as accommodating only the river flowing under the railway, the order must have left the tank commanders distinctly puzzled.[3]

It was, however, cancelled later the same day, with the admission that 'from later reconnaissance of the ground, it has been found impracticable to use the routes given for the tanks'. Instead, all four were now to move up to the railway line, two then proceeding to the left and two to the right, and subsequently to make every endeavour to cross the river with the help of the Engineers, and reach the Beaucourt–Miraumont road. If unable to cross, they were to remain on the line of the railway and assist the infantry assault in any way they could.

Haig eventually decided that the operations outlined here (and those in V Corps which we will examine later) were altogether too ambitious and he called for a scaled-down version in which the 4th Canadian and 18th Divisions, together with their accompanying tanks, were to play no part.

Instead, 39th Division was to launch an assault from the northern edge of Schwaben Redoubt with all four battalions of 118th Brigade in the line – 1st Hertfordshire, 1st Cambridgeshire, 6th Cheshire and 4/5th Black Watch. These were to advance over ground lying mainly to their north-west, down to the Ancre Valley and the German defences which lined the road along it. Three tanks here were to be supported by a subsidiary infantry attack launched from the lower portion of Mill Road by 16th Sherwood Foresters (Notts. and Derby) of 117th Brigade. The tanks were to destroy all enemy positions along the Ancre up to and including St Pierre Divion and then to seize Bridge Road, which led north over the river and railway. Thereafter they were to be protected on their right by 19th Division wheeling on its hinge near Stump Road.

These arrangements were set out in instructions dated 25 October but the continuing bad weather imposed repeated delays and the new date eventually decided on for the attack was 13 November. Clearly the task was not going to be easy. The Germans defending St Pierre Divion were still holding out despite the more than four months of fighting which had elapsed since the Battle of the Somme opened on 1 July. They were well established in deep dug-outs and emplacements along the minor road leading from Mill Road to the village and beyond.

Three tanks of A Company, probably all drawn from its no. 3 Section but designated A, B and C for the purpose of this operation, were assigned to support the attack. Tank A was to proceed to the Strassburg Line at point R19a 4.5, go down part way to the village, then return to R19a 6.8, where it was to swing up Serb Road towards the Hansa Line. Here it was to turn left and follow the trench almost down to the road below, where new orders would be given to it. These would call for it either to attack targets in the valley or to press on to Grandcourt.

Tank B's task was to advance along the enemy support line as far as Q24b 7.1, turn north-east, then enter St Pierre Divion from the east. After the capture of the village it was to go to R13c 3.8 and assist in seizing the crossing over the Ancre at Q18b 8.3.

However, neither of these tanks was able to carry out its orders. One of them broke a gear and the other sank into the mud soon after starting.[4]

At 5.45 a.m., in darkness and fog, the surviving Tank C, no. 544, bearing the company designation A13, left the assembly point at Paisley Dump, Q30c 7.3, adjacent to the track called Speyside Road on the south side of Thiepval Wood. It then ground its way up Paisley Avenue on the wood's south-eastern side, and reached the German defences on its north-eastern side at around 7 a.m. By now its commander, Lieutenant H.W. Hitchcock, must have known, if he did not know before, that his two would-be companions were not with him, but, nothing daunted, he proceeded along the enemy front line, crushing the wire as he went, and continued to the point where the line terminated in machine-gun emplacements at Q24b 1.1, down near the river. By destroying these he would be easing the passage of the four battalions of 118th Brigade attacking from the south-east and that of the 16th Sherwood Foresters waiting in the mists by Mill Road for the moment to move up in support.

The first stretch of the minor road branching off from Mill Road towards St Pierre Divion was judged to be impassable due to shell-holes and felled trees. Also, in the embankment alongside it there were several entrances leading into a massive system of tunnels and underground chambers capable of housing and equipping hundreds of German troops. The instructions issued to Hitchcock before the battle had therefore called on him to bypass all this by retracing his steps up to Q24b 5.0, then to turn north along the higher ground. From there he was to drop down to the road again in order to deal with a strong-point located in houses at Q24b 5.4 and also a trench leading to the Summer House[5] near a foot-bridge over the Ancre. Further instructions were to be given to him when he reached the church in St Pierre Divion, and would almost certainly have called on him to continue on to Bridge Road and help secure the bridge over the Ancre opposite Beaucourt Station, which was a task assigned to the now-missing Tank B.[6]

RFC reports show that Hitchcock followed the first part of his orders fairly closely, but he was destined not to complete the rest. A13 had already encountered one problem crossing no-man's-land when its tracks had failed for a moment or two to get a grip on the soggy ground. It had eventually freed itself but the trouble occurred again here on the enemy's front trench at Q24d 6.8. The machine now seemed to be stuck fast and the 16th Sherwood Foresters were still some way behind, whereas the enemy were extremely close.

In a report written the following day, based largely on an account by the tank's second in command, Corporal Taffs, the officer commanding A Company described what followed:

Up till now none of our troops had been seen and the car was surrounded by the enemy. About this time Lieutenant Hitchcock was wounded in the head and gave orders to abandon the car, and then handed over the command to Corporal Taffs. Three men and Lieutenant Hitchcock got out of the car; Lieutenant Hitchcock was seen to fall at once, but no more was seen of two of the three men who had evacuated the tank. The third man was pulled back into the tank after he had been wounded in the forearm, and as the enemy were shooting through the open door it was immediately closed. Fire was at once opened upon the enemy, who retired to cover and returned fire with machine-guns and rifles.

Corporal Taffs decided not to abandon the tank but with the help of the driver, Lance Corporal Bevan, who had been previously wounded about the face by splinters from his [*lookout*] prism, to carry on and try to get the tank forward to its objective. They managed to extricate the vehicle by using the reverse [*gear*] and then drove forward as far as the German second line where the tank crashed into a dug-out at Q24b 8.1 and was hopelessly engulfed, lying at an angle of about 45 degrees, thereby causing the two guns on the lower side to be useless and the two guns on the upper side only capable of firing at a high angle.

The tank was now attacked by the Germans with machine guns and also bombed from the sides, front and underneath. At about 8 a.m., as none of our troops had as yet been seen, probably owing to the thick mist which prevailed during the whole action, Corporal Taffs sent a message by carrier pigeon asking for assistance.[7]

'Help at once. Am in German line ditched. Signed Corporal Taffs.'

This was received by II Corps who passed it on to the 11th Infantry Brigade, who gave orders to the Black Watch to render all assistance possible. At about 9 a.m. the tank was relieved by a party of the Notts. and Derby Regiment who were soon followed by the Black Watch. Corporal Taffs and the remainder of the crew left the tank when our line was established well in front of it and it was safe from capture by the enemy.

The bodies of Lieutenant Hitchcock and Gunner Miles were found and identified today. Gunner Stanley was seen being conveyed to hospital after the action. The guns have been removed from the tank by a salvage party today and brought back to camp.

The crew of the tank were:

In command:	Lt Hitchcock H.W.	Killed
40429	Cpl Taffs, A.	
M2/106388	L/Cpl Bevan R.	Wounded
32092	L/Cpl Moss, S.A.	
38166	Gnr Stanley, W.A.	Wounded
40066	Gnr Miles, W.J.	Killed
32175	Gnr Ainley, F.	Wounded[8]
38046	Gnr Tolley, A.W.	

Corporal Taffs and the men who remained in the tank with him undoubtedly did splendid work by remaining at their posts. I would especially bring to notice the names of 40429 Corporal Taffs and M2/106388 Lance Corporal Bevan.

Signed C.M. Tippetts, Major, Commanding A Company Heavy Section, MGC

14/11/16

Taffs was awarded the Military Medal, as were Bevan, Moss, Ainley and Tolley. The citation reads:

> These men formed the crew of a tank operating against St Pierre Divion on 13 November 1916. Brought up under very difficult conditions, theirs was the only tank to start, and penetrated to the second enemy support line.[9] Here, for more than an hour, they maintained their position without assistance, their infantry having lost touch owing to the heavy mist. The officer in charge was killed while endeavouring to establish touch. Corporal Taffs then took command and Lance Corporal Bevan drove on another 200 yards, when the tank was ditched in a German dug-out. The crew worked under fire for over two hours, endeavouring to extricate it. Finding this impossible, they attached themselves to a battalion of the Black Watch and assisted them in mopping up the position.

Photographs of this tank taken after the battle show the name *We're all in it* painted on its side. If this was indeed its name, then clearly it did not follow the practice elsewhere in the Heavy Section of bearing a name starting with the company letter – in this case A. Other tanks in A Company did so (although some commanders chose not to have one at all), and at least by the summer of 1917, when the Tank Corps was formed, A Battalion had a tank A13 named *Auxiliary,* albeit a different machine, a male, no. 767. We believe, however, that the name shown in the photograph must have been applied after the battle when some enterprising soldier, equipped with a paintbrush and a sense of humour, carefully matched the style of name adopted on other tanks in order to demonstrate the irony of A13's demise. We believe that the name *We're all in it* may have been the title of a song popular at the time but we cannot provide evidence for this. We do know, however, that a song of that name was written in the Second World War – a curious coincidence.

There is no mention in Taffs' account of the infantry 'guard' of one NCO and two men which, according to orders issued by II Corps, each tank was supposed to carry with it into battle. It would seem that the idea was dropped, no doubt because of space considerations. Some sort of infantry escort may indeed have been allocated to each tank but the men in that case would have travelled on foot, not in the tank, and were probably no more than the parties of infantry employed elsewhere to clear wounded men from the path of each machine.[10]

Later actions

As a follow-up to 39th Division's attack, and in a continued attempt to meet the aims laid down in Fifth Army Operational Order 32 of 15 October,[11] 18th and 19th Divisions went into action in a separate operation mounted on 18 November and achieved some success, reportedly without the aid of tanks which, because of the mud, had now been rendered useless.

Further to the right, in the area of the East Miraumont Road, the Canadians, too, met with success, albeit at some cost. We know that their troops operating here included a group of eight signallers in 50th Battalion, one of whom, Victor Wheeler, has left an account of the battle that day. He describes how, under a hail of machine-gun fire, 77mm and howitzer shells, he and a companion made their way forward through the dust and smoke:

> Our objective was a wrecked British Mark I Swinton tank, immobilised on a distant knoll. It was aflame like a huge Olympic torch, lighting the tortured landscape for half a mile in all directions. For the past thirty-six hours billowing clouds of yellowish black-tinged, oily smoke, like fumes pouring from the stacks of a mammoth steel-mill, had steadily risen hundreds of feet into the air . . . As Jack and I, who were on the extreme right of our battalion, gradually separated ourselves from the main line of advancing Canucks, we came upon a partially hidden tank that had been battered to a Dante-esque standstill by a direct hit. A closer look at the iron monster, a lozenge-shaped land-dreadnought, revealed the annihilated crew, one officer and seven O.R.s, spilled out of the once-chugging steel fortress. Only two members of the lifeless crew were whole, but they were deeply lacerated, as if by vicious pinking shears, and blackened by the still burning tank-oil that had smoked their clothes. One young lad, ashen as sun-bleached bones, was cruelly splashed with his own jelling blood. Other prostrate figures were grotesquely mutilated by the tank explosion. They lay stiffening in a zig-zag chain, one man's outstretched hand trying to grasp the next man's bootless foot, and that corpse, in turn, reaching to clutch another's bandoleer.[12]

Wheeler's account makes it clear that he saw *two* wrecked tanks in this area, the one that he evidently approached close enough to see its dead crewmen, and the other burning away in the distance. He and Jack continued their progress beyond the first and on towards this further objective, despite barbed wire and the machine-gun fire being aimed at them, until a party of fifty advancing Germans followed by an even larger force obliged them to make a hasty withdrawal.

But of interest is his statement that the tank on the 'distant knoll' had been burning for thirty-six hours, which – assuming that his timing was accurate – puts its demise back to the evening of the 16th. We assume that the 'partially hidden' tank which he had viewed at close quarters had been destroyed at roughly the same time.

However, the presence of tanks here, again supposing Wheeler's account to be correct, is passed over in silence in all the other documents that we have seen. We know, of course, that Haig had decided to reduce the scale of the

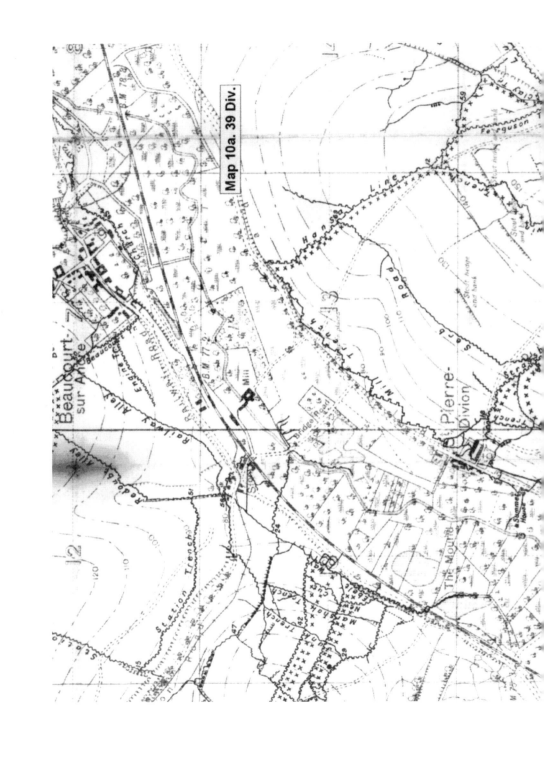

Map 10a. 39 Div.

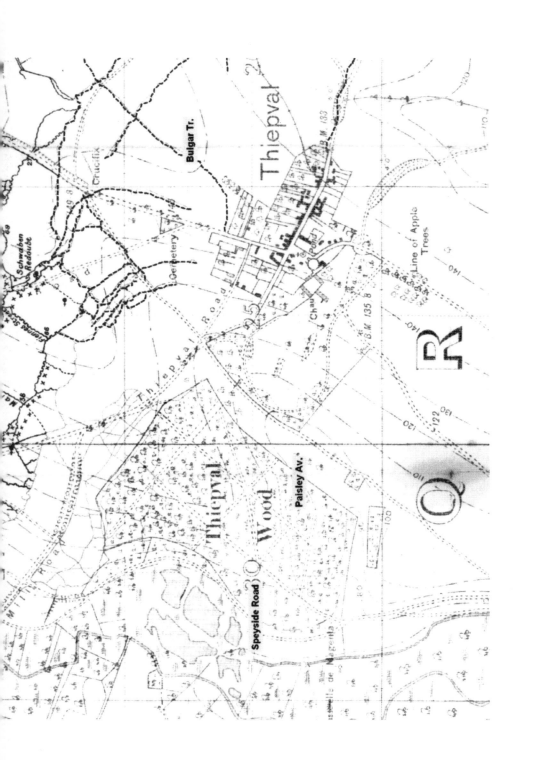

II Corps attack on 13 November, which was originally to employ seventeen tanks (all in A Company), by simply standing down 19th and 18th Divisions, with their four and ten tanks respectively, and using only 39th Division, which had three.

We also know that the earlier plan called for 18th Division to detach one of its ten machines to accompany the 4th Canadian Division fighting alongside it, east of the East Miraumont Road, but if subsequent instructions ruled that no tanks were to be used in this area after the 13th – which we believe to be the case – can Wheeler's story about tanks in the Canadian sector be true? It is not unknown, after all, for soldiers in any war to exaggerate – even invent – accounts of their adventures.

There is some evidence that his account may be accurate, at least in part, for we have the picture of a tank entitled *The First Tank – Somme 1916 August* [sic]. It bears the name of the artist, Major Walter Keesey, who apparently drew it in 1917. The tank is identified in the bottom left-hand corner of the drawing as *Ariadne*, so it clearly belonged to A Company. Also shown, circled, are the names of Le Sars on the left and Martinpuich on the right, their respective bearings indicating that the tank was positioned north of the Albert–Bapaume road, the artist looking to the south-east. Additionally, the tank must have been east of the East Miraumont Road, probably some distance north of Dyke Road in the valley (Vallée du Sars on the IGN map) which lies near Courcelette.

Although Wheeler says that there were two wrecked tanks in this area, we have no explanation for the existence of a second tank, except to mention – only to discount it – a reference in both the British and Canadian *Official Histories* to the problems caused by a smokescreen laid down in advance of the attacking force. But since Wheeler himself refers to this we can be sure that he did not think this was the source of the flame and smoke which he describes as emanating from the tank on the knoll.

In brief then, although the tank on the knoll remains a mystery, we are as sure as we can be that at least *Ariadne* was in the area described.

So why was there no official mention of its presence in the battle? We can only speculate, until some firmer evidence emerges, that the Canadians were at some late stage given permission to use their one allotted tank, and possibly another, on or just before the 18th, in recognition of the more difficult task facing them on the flank of the attack, but that they decided not to mention the fact in their subsequent reporting. Security and secrecy may have been considerations in this decision, for there is evidence that various other units, even in the late autumn of 1916 when the existence of tanks was widely known, were reluctant to refer openly in their reports to the existence of these new 'cars'.

Field Guide

IGN Maps 2407E & 2407O

To see where the tanks were to operate with the Canadians, go first to Courcelette and take the D107 signposted to Miraumont, known in 1916 as the East Miraumont Road. (The West Miraumont Road, for most of its way, is not much more than a cart-track.) As you leave the village you will see on your right a depression, Vallée du Sars, known in 1916 as Dyke Valley. Somewhere in the fields beyond its northern rim, and possibly beyond the Germans' former North Practice Trenches, is where *Ariadne* was hit and where Wheeler says he found the bodies of its crew strewn around the wreck.

For Stuff Redoubt, drive towards Miraumont but before reaching the railway arch turn left along the D151 into Grandcourt. In the centre of the village turn left onto the road, a continuation of the D151, signposted to Thiepval. This bends round and upwards and after 600m leads towards a crossroads where Stump Road turns up to the left – a very sunken road indeed. You first pass Stump Road Cemetery on the left, then arrive at the access path to Grandcourt Road Cemetery on the right. The graves here lie on the rearmost of the parallel trenches of Feste Stauffen as shown on German maps but British maps clearly show the redoubt as a rhomboid further south, occupying space on the 2006 IGN map enclosed by spot heights 153 and 156 and the word *Terroir*.[13] The start point for Captain Raikes' attack on Grandcourt was to be R21a 4.7, a point along the continuation of Stuff Trench 200m north-east of the cemetery.

The best way to see the site of Paisley Dump, Q30c 7.3, is similar to the route suggested in the chapter on Thiepval. Take the road leading out of Authuille towards Thiepval but follow this only for a couple of hundred metres. From here take the track leading off to the left which eventually brings you to the edge of Thiepval Wood. The start point for A13 and its companions was only a few metres from the track that you are on.

To see where A13 was ditched go to the Ulster Tower, the monument erected to commemorate the men of the 36th (Ulster) Division who fought here during the first few days of the battle in July. Leave your car by the entrance and walk down the track in the fields on the left for 380m, and Q24b 8.1 is about 40m on your left. The place where A13 was first halted, Q24d 6.8, is half-way back to the main road in a roughly south-south-westerly direction.

---

[1]   The Quadrilateral lay where the double trenches of the Gallwitz Riegel (a continuation of the Gird Line) were crossed by the double trenches of the Below Stellung (a continuation of the Flers Line).

[2]   The History of B Company, held in the archives at Bovington, says that this happened on the Courcelette–Pozieres road but this is narrow and winding

whereas a photograph shows a relatively broad, straight highway readily recognisable as the main Albert–Bapaume D929. This, too, can be thought of as linking the two villages as Courcelette lies only a short distance to its north. In a letter to the Official Historian in 1934, General Sir Hugh Elles confirmed that the incident took place 'near the Pozières–Le Sars road'.

3   19th Division's G.54/6/10b of 25 October.

4   Tanks A and B were probably commanded by Lieutenants Houghton and Munro-Phillips, the other two officers of A Company's no. 3 Section.

5   This was perhaps the ruin of a pre-war building but equally possibly a German emplacement owing its name to the British soldiers' sense of irony.

6   Paragraph 6 of the instructions given to the tank commanders said: 'In the case of one tank breaking down or only two tanks being available, the two remaining tanks will carry out the tasks allotted to Tanks B and C.' Understandably, the nearer targets were to be given priority.

7   The text of this message was in the War Diary, not in Major Tippetts' report.

8   Clearly Ainley was the wounded man pulled back into the tank.

9   The sequence is wrong. Lieutenant Hitchcock and the others got out of the tank on the first German line. It was Taffs who took it on to the second line.

10   On 15 September 1916 three tanks of C Company (C2, C4 and C6) each carried nine men into battle. The intended role of the ninth man is not known.

11   See earlier in this chapter.

12   Passage quoted by Paul Reed in *Courcelette* (Pen & Sword Books).

13   'Terroir' has nothing to do with terror. The term is used to define a locality, with special reference to its agricultural products.

Chapter 11

Beaumont Hamel (North): October and November

We saw in the previous chapter that Haig's plan for offensive action in October and November immediately south of the Ancre called for an advance by II Corps, and initially also by the Canadian Corps, from their start point on the Thiepval Ridge down to the river on a front extending from Thiepval itself along to a point east of Courcelette. In this and the next chapter we look at the work of V Corps, extending from a point well north of Beaumont Hamel, and eventually down as far as the right bank of the river immediately opposite II Corps.

The origin of this part of Haig's plan lay in a visit which he paid to Reserve Army headquarters on 20 September, when he instructed Gough to prepare plans for capturing the Serre ridge by an attack with infantry and tanks advancing along a front extending from the Redan Ridge up to Hébuterne.

Bearing in mind that this instruction was given to Gough just five days after the tanks' first ever employment in battle, when their success was considered by some to be no more than partial, it demonstrates a remarkable faith on Haig's part in the new weapon of war and in its potential for the future.

Equally surprising perhaps is Haig's instruction to General Allenby, Gough's neighbour to the north, during the Commander-in-Chief's visit to him at Third Army headquarters on 24 September:

> I directed Allenby to make preparations to attack Gommecourt with the object of holding that place and the ridge running south-east to cover the left of an attack by General Gough eastwards from the 'Sunken Road' through Serre and Puisieux upon Achiet-le-Grand… For this operation Allenby would have three divisions, and if necessary a fourth, and twelve to twenty-five tanks (a company). My intention is (if the attack comes off) to make it by surprise with a line of fifty or sixty tanks and no artillery bombardment.

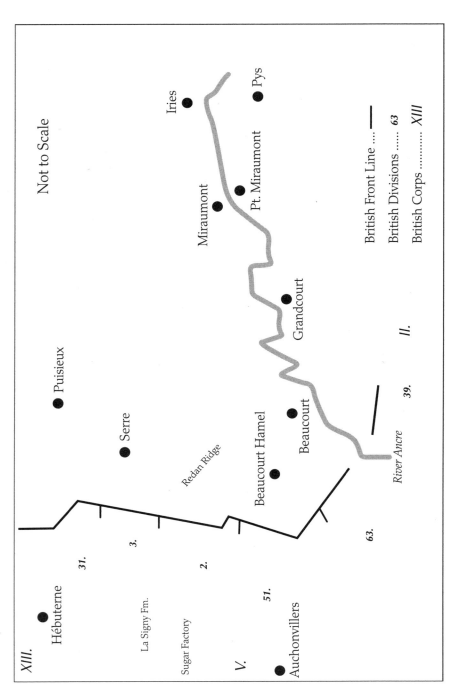

Map 11. The Battle of the Somme: The Ancre, 13 November 1916.

This last sentence refers, of course, to Gough's attack, not Allenby's, but it later became clear that the number of tanks available was not, after all, sufficient to support operations as far north as Gommecourt. Haig therefore promptly excluded Allenby's Third Army from his plans and called instead for Gough's northern flank, advancing on a front between John Copse[1] and Hébuterne, to be protected by his own XIII Corps, but still with assistance from the Heavy Section.

D Company

The tanks selected to work with XIII Corps were those of of D Company and on 2 October Major Frank Summers was briefed on plans for his role in the attack. Although the number of available machines estimated earlier was to prove wildly optimistic, extensive preparations were made. Summers duly went to Hébuterne on 3 October to see the layout of trenches and the condition of the ground. He went again the following day, this time accompanied by Captain Mortimore, and selected a site for the company 'dump' of stores and one for the company headquarters. Preliminary preparations were also made for the reception of the tanks. On 7 October Mortimore conducted his fellow officers there to examine the boundaries, landmarks, etc, but while there they came under shell-fire which resulted in Lieutenant Bown being slightly wounded and later evacuated. Throughout the following period further visits were made to the area to view possible points of assembly and routes up to the front line. Lieutenant Enoch appears to have been the officer in charge of organising the construction of dug-outs for officers and men and of 'stables' for the tanks soon to be brought forward.

Following the fall of Morval, Combles, Gueudecourt, Flers, Martinpuich, Courcelette and Thiepval, GHQ's OAD 159 of 29 September had decreed that all available tanks – those in Fourth Army south of the Albert–Bapaume road and those in Reserve Army north of it – were to be collected together for Gough's operations north of the Ancre. In the event, as we know, not all of them were despatched. Some of the earlier casualties were still out on the battlefield, damaged beyond recovery, while others were being repaired, a task made more difficult by the shortage of skilled labour.[2] Also, provision had to be made for future operations now being planned, such as that of Bown and Wakley at Eaucourt l'Abbaye and Bell at Le Sars. There were other tanks left at Green Dump near Longueval and some at the Loop (the railhead near Bray-sur-Somme) but eight were eventually released by Fourth Army in response to Haig's instructions.

The first day of October was fine and clear, but the following week saw frequent showers, which made the ground dangerously soft. Nonetheless planning had to go ahead in the hope that a dry spell would eventually return, but in the evening of 6 October most of the officers and crews were taken back by bus and lorry to the newly constructed 'tankodrome' at Acheux-en-Amiénois, 6 miles north-west of Albert. There was little for them to do in the forward zone.

C Company

On 8 October, while the officers of D Company were engaged in their preparations around Hébuterne, the commanding officer of C Company, Major Allen Holford-Walker, attended a meeting at the headquarters of V Corps to discuss preparations for the part that his own tanks were to play in the renewed attack on the German lines, closer to Beaumont Hamel. He was shown maps indicating the various Objectives and the routes which it was thought the tanks should follow in order to reach them. On his return he outlined these plans to C Company's tank commanders in his Operational Order no. 5 issued that same afternoon. Each officer came back from Acheux to spend time reconnoitring the routes chosen and reporting on the work that needed to be done in order to make them viable. The weather was still showery but the forecast was now more optimistic.

The plans called for just ten machines to take part in this sector, of which six were later allocated to Captain Clively, working with 3rd Division in three pairs or 'groups' designated A, B and C, and four to Captain Hiscocks, working with 2nd Division in two pairs, D and E.

On Z Day – the exact date was still to be announced – the tanks were to leave the tankodrome on the night of W/X for Beaussart (map reference P11b), where they would spend the whole of X Day. On the night of X/Y they would proceed to their place of assembly at K27d 1.4, which lay 320m west of La Signy Farm. Here the tanks would spend the whole of Y Day, while the crews themselves would be withdrawn to the rear, leaving the tanks with a small guard to keep away the inquisitive. The crews, having enjoyed a few hours' rest, would return during the evening and then, between 6.30 p.m. and 10.30 p.m. of Y/Z night, would drive along previously reconnoitred routes to their respective start points nearer the front line. Each group's subsequent route across the enemy's lines was shown on a map, as were the various Objectives which each was required to reach.

Holford-Walker's HQ at the start of the battle was to be at K28c 1½.1, later amended to K28c 2.2, co-located with 3rd Division's Advanced HQ, 140m south-east of La Signy. Clively's HQ was to be at K28b 4½.1, 90m south-east of Observation Wood, and therefore near the junction of Landward Trench with Dunmow Trench. Hiscocks' was to be at K34b 0.1, co-located with the HQ of 5th Infantry Brigade in Vallade Trench, 365m behind the front line, immediately north of the road leading towards this from the Sugar Factory.

Following a further conference on 9 October, V Corps published its own GX 7618/22, which repeated much of what Holford-Walker had already reported.

It added that the tanks would start at Zero, and would therefore be behind the infantry to begin with, but at a forecast speed of 20 yards a minute they would 'probably overtake the infantry at the First Objective'. Given the state of the ground, this was optimistic, even if slower than ¾ mph. However, this day was the first of eight or nine marked by dry, often sunny weather, and the prospects for success began to look increasingly good.

Other matters covered in this order, and in the later GX 7618/39 of 12 October, included the need to bridge or 'ramp' the British trenches to be crossed; the need for one infantry NCO and six men to accompany each tank to remove the wounded from its path; the need for the infantry to understand the methods of operation of the tanks and what they were capable of; and what their crews' various signals were intended to convey. To mask the sound of the tanks' engines there would be

> a noise demonstration carried out by artillery, trench mortars, machine gun and rifle fire, and by some flying and bomb dropping by aeroplanes. Tanks can only be heard from about 500 yards away and a great deal of noise will not be necessary. In order to drill the enemy to it, this noise demonstration will be carried out on 13th, 15th and 16th October from 8.30 p.m. to 10.30 p.m. [*later amended to 7 p.m. to 10 p.m.*] Although the primary object is to produce noise, these drill demonstrations will be designed to inflict as much damage as possible on the enemy at those places most advantageous from the point of view of the attack.

The staff of 2nd Division called on its brigade and artillery commanders to submit to it any proposals they might have on the matter of cooperation with the tanks and any questions that they wished put to the tank officers.

A 'dump' was set up at Beaussart and a larger one further forward near the tanks' place of assembly at K27d 1.4 in Jeremiah Lane, west of La Signy. This latter facility eventually contained all that was deemed necessary to keep the tanks in action during the operation – 2000 gallons of petrol, 160 gallons of Zeta heavy oil, 300 gallons of Heavy Steam Cylinder oil, 300 pounds of grease and 40 gallons of Mobiloil. Stocks of ammunition were also to be placed here – 480 rounds of 6-pdr shells, 50,000 rounds of .303 for the machine guns and 1,000 rounds of .45 for revolvers.

On 10 October eleven new tanks arrived at the Loop railhead. Unfortunately two of these were destroyed by fire when moving up to the battle zone two days later.[3] The result of the subsequent court of inquiry is not on record but, whatever the circumstances, the incident did not prevent four more tanks being added to the proposed attacking force in this area on 12 October. Hiscocks, in 2nd Division's sector, acquired all four of the new machines and formed them into two groups, F and G, which he added to E, but in exchange he gave up his group D to Clively, working with 3rd Division.

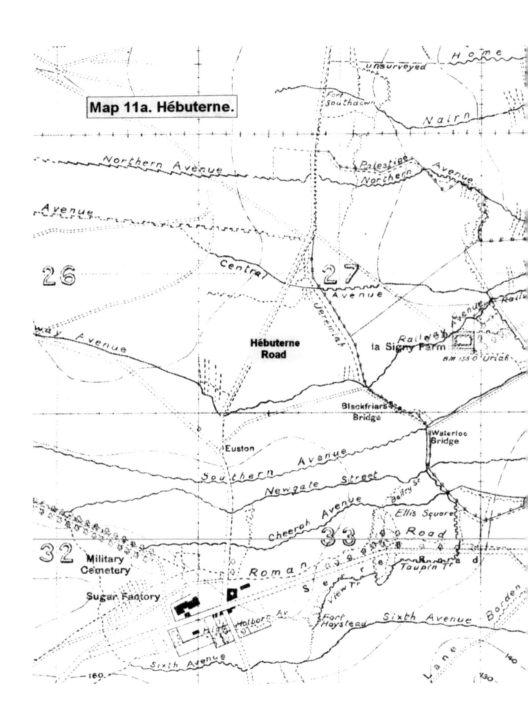

Map 11a. Hébuterne.

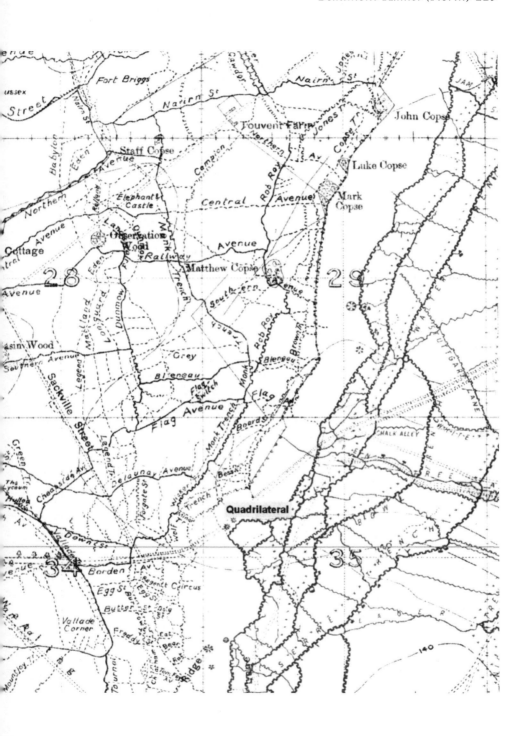

The point of assembly of groups A, B, C, D and E was confirmed as K27d 1.4 in Jeremiah Lane, whereas that of groups F and G was to be K33c 2.8, beside the Hébuterne road just north of the Sugar Factory. While stationed at these places, the greatest care was to be taken to camouflage all the tanks with tarpaulins smeared with mud and covered with leaves.

At 10 p.m. on the evening of 10 October experiments were carried out at Acheux to find out just how liable to discovery the tanks would be, either from the sound of their engines or visually from flares, as they assembled in the dark before attacking. Very lights were used, and these showed that the tanks remained invisible at anything over 320m from the light source, but the motors could be clearly heard at 450m.

The following days were put to good use by the attached pioneers, stalwart men of the Monmouthshire Regiment, building the crossing points to be negotiated by the tanks when advancing over the British trenches. Frustratingly, some of these 'bridges', once built, had to be demolished and replaced by others elsewhere owing to the state of the ground or because of competing priorities in the areas selected. Further reconnaissance by the tank commanders also led to some alterations in the routes.

What must have been even more frustrating was the announcement by Reserve Army in its Operational Order 32 of 15 October cancelling all the preparations so far made and substituting a new plan, Haig having decided to concentrate his efforts in a more limited area, leaving no portion of the attacking line under-manned. 3rd Division and 2nd Division, opposite the rising ground of Serre and the Redan, were the least affected, but 31st Division, the only division remaining in XIII Corps following the transfer of its 19th Division to II Corps and of its 51st (Highland) Division to V Corps, was now to do little more than provide a perforce less powerful protective flank for the men of V Corps setting out from the front line on their right. At the same time D Company of the Heavy Section yielded to C Company its flank protection role here, then 'leapfrogged' over it to establish itself in the village of Beaumont Hamel and the ground to its south down as far as the Ancre. Here it was to support 51st Division and also the 63rd (Royal Naval) Division.

So the intention now was to concentrate all available forces in II Corps south of the river and V Corps north of it in an attack aimed at capturing an area bounded by the East Miraumont Road, the villages of Petit Miraumont and Miraumont itself, the Beauregard Dovecote, then along the high ground running back to the west through Serre. Later targets would include Pys and Irles. As we have seen in the previous chapter, these plans allowed for II Corps to employ twenty tanks and V Corps to employ twenty-five. A further fifteen, it was said, might later be made available.

Although many of the tankmen must have looked forward to putting on a good 'show' as a result of this reorganisation, others must have been apprehensive about the danger of it turning into a 'flop' in front of a watchful audience both in France and in London. The period 9–16 October had proved bright and mainly dry but thereafter heavy rain set in and lasted almost to the end of the month. The ground, already torn and battered by shells, became swampy and treacherous underfoot, conditions which augured badly for the infantry whose task was to cross it under enemy fire. As for the tanks, it began to look doubtful if they could ever get to the British front line, let alone across no-man's-land and the even more devastated ground of the German defences.

We will describe the actions of the D Company tanks in a later chapter, but let us first continue here with an account of C Company's work.

The northern flank was not, after all, forgotten. When a new pair of tanks arrived on 16 October they were briefly assigned to Hiscocks' sector, but were then switched on 18 October to operate under Captain Archie Holford-Walker, brother of the CO, with 31st Division in the XIII Corps sector. They were given no identifying letter.

Allen Holford-Walker confirmed these arrangements in his Operational Order no. 6 of 22 October, while Appendix 12 of the War Diary added the group letters and names of the commanders of all sixteen tanks taking part. It also gave the serial numbers of various other tanks, positioned in other corps areas south of the Ancre, but without identifying details.

Captain Clively: 3rd Division

A	758 Hallack		B	511 Clarke
	549 Atherton			521 Mills
C	744 Reardon		D	523 Lambert
	528 Groves			514 Williamson

Captain Hiscocks: 2nd Division

E	706 Arnaud		F	766 Thompson
	524 Murphy			522 Ambrose
G	710 Bates			
	505 (sic, or 507) Elliot			

Captain Holford-Walker: 31st Division (XIII Corps)
561 Captain Bennewith; 772 Captain Lord Rodney (both officers attached from B Company, recently arrived in France less tanks)

Captain Inglis: XIV, III and II Corps
505 (sic, see Elliot above), 533, 554, 703, 705, 722, 740, 741, 746, 760.

The same Order also pointed out that the ultimate objective of the tanks operating with 2nd and 3rd Divisions was to be Puisieux Trench, L20, 26 and 32 and south to R2, over 2750m behind the German front line.

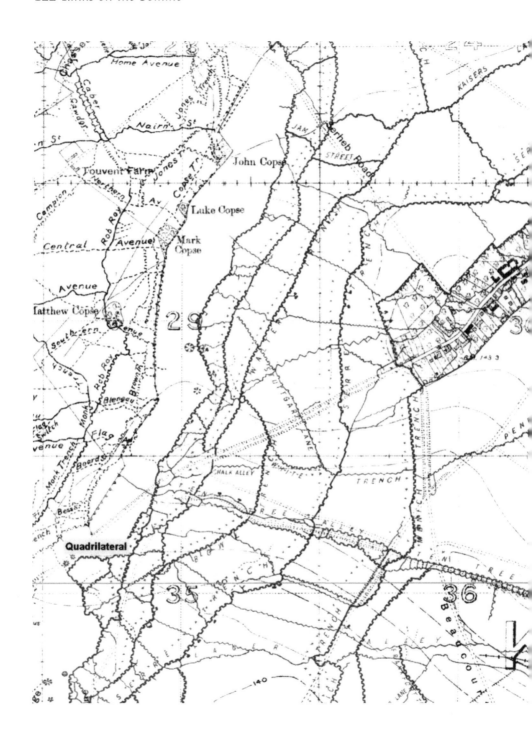

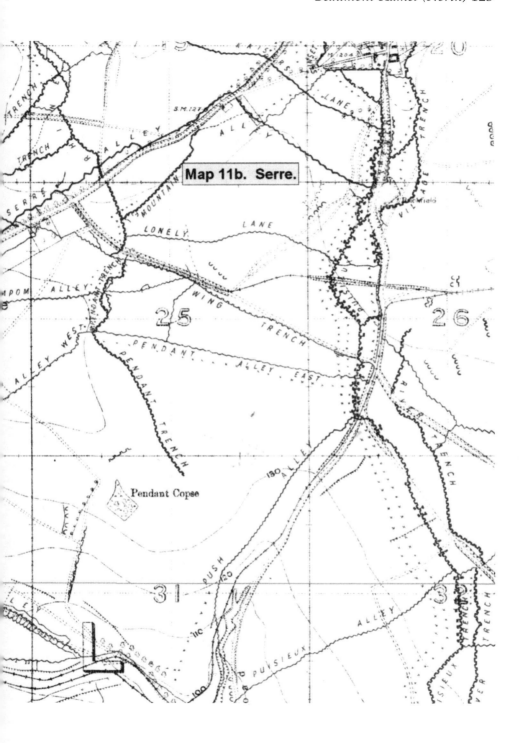

Map 11b. Serre.

Pendant Copse

In a rare reference to the officer commanding the whole tank force now stationed in France, Lieutenant-Colonel Bradley, a movement order issued on 22 October mentions that on the night of Y/Z his HQ was to move forward to Observation Point no. 2 of V Corps, closer to the front line. We believe this may have been at the Lyceum, at the north end of Vallade Trench. At the same time Holford-Walker's C Company HQ would move up to the Advanced HQ of 3rd Division at K28c 2.2.

These moves, however, did not take place, at least not yet, for a decision was taken on 23 October to postpone operations by 24 hours. The following day a postponement of a further 48 hours was ordered, but this did not, of course, interrupt the preparations being made. Men and materials were sent forward from Acheux to establish 'Halfway House' at Beaussart.

On 25 October C Company issued Holford-Walker's Operational Order no. 7 announcing that, 2nd Division being required to attack along a front extending from Q4b 7.0 (originally 7.9, later changed) to K35a 4.9, C Company's tanks here would form up behind Wolf, Wicker and Monk trenches in its immediate rear. In 3rd Division, attacking along a front extending from K35a 4.9 to John Copse, its tanks would form up behind Rob Roy Trench. Further north, the tanks with 31st Division of XIII Corps would start from John Copse.

The order made it clear that tanks were to move on from the various Objectives at the same time as the infantry, but nowhere were they to precede the infantry unless by doing so they could help them forward. They and the infantry were to keep as close as possible to the 'creeping' barrage.

These Objectives, or 'phases' of the attack, were the First (Green Line), Second (Yellow Line), Third (Blue Line) and Fourth (Brown Line), these being sited between the British front line and Beauregard Dovecote. The importance of this feature – *beauregard* can be translated as 'fine view' – derived from its dominating position on high ground north of Miraumont, where a prominent pigeon-house was located. Its capture, which now became the Fifth Objective, was to be undertaken by a single brigade loaned for the purpose from 37th Division, hitherto held in Corps reserve but now placed under the command of 2nd Division.

The final objective of 2nd Division itself was the double line of the Puisieux and River Trenches (often referred to as a single defensive system, the Puisieux River Trench) extending from R2b 2.9 to L32b 0.8 and the subsequent formation of a defensive flank running forward along the high ground to Beauregard Dovecote, once this had been captured by 37th Division.

For 3rd Division, the Final Objective was a defensive flank facing north along the Brown Line, i.e. L26c 9.0 to L25a 4.9 to K30a 1.9. In other respects its orders, at least for the tanks, were the same as those for 2nd Division.

The plan outlined above was substantially re-worded in an amendment – hastily drafted it would seem – sent out later in the day by Holford-Walker. Evidently responding to an urgent demand from higher authority, he warned his tank commanders that they would now have to accompany the infantry all the way to the area up to and beyond the Dovecote, to a new Objective to be called the Pink Line. Glancing at their maps, they would have been dismayed to discover that the furthest point of this line lay 5.5km from their start point. This was a long way for thirsty tanks and tired crews.

> All tanks must hold themselves in readiness to assist the 2nd and 37th Divisions in their attack on the Pink Line. Time of advance is Zero plus 4 hours and 50 minutes.
>
> On the attack on the Pink Line starting, tanks working with 3rd Division (i.e. A, B, C and D groups) should proceed up the road L32b 4.9 – Beauregard Alley – Pigeon Lane to the attack on Beauregard Dovecote, a proportion of available tanks being sent north to isolate it and to block the sunken road at L28c 9.7, while a proportion [*goes*] south to cut it off from Miraumont. They should clear the Y road in L34.
>
> Tanks working with 2nd Division, i.e. E, F and G groups, should proceed via Swan Trench and Hindenburg Trench, clearing sunken roads, to attack Miraumont from the west. They will be assisted by 3rd Division tanks from the north after the capture of the Dovecote. The senior tank officer on the spot must decide on the sub-division of tanks for the attack on the Pink Line.

With this clarification, C Company's preparations for battle were now almost complete, although the uncertain weather meant that no date for the attack had yet been announced. But at least objectives had been specified, routes laid down, timings noted, dumps of rations and ammunition filled. For its part, 2nd Division had given the infantry useful advice about the tank's capabilities and shortcomings, warning that it

> . . . must be regarded as nearly blind and deaf. It can, however, communicate by hanging out flags as follows: Red = Broken down, Green = Am on objective. In order to facilitate communication with aircraft, arrangements will be made by the Officer Commanding 2/Signal Company for one signaller to be carried in each tank. This signaller will operate a lamp through the roof and will send and receive messages. It is important that signallers should be on the lookout for signals from aircraft as it is from aircraft that the most reliable information is received as to the position of our infantry.

It is not known whether this idea was ever put into practice. It is, however, certain that the proposal for each tank to be accompanied by an infantry escort was carried out, its task being to clear wounded men out of the path of the tank and also to watch for infantry signals to the tank which it would relay to the crew via the rear door, left unlocked for the purpose. Men of these escorts had, of course, an unenviable task. To walk in front of something against which every German field gun and machine gun was aimed cannot have been an appealing prospect.

For good measure, several days of heavy showers had now transformed the ground into a quagmire, which days of occasional brief sunshine had been unable to dry out thoroughly. On the 24th conditions worsened; showers now turned into a steady downpour which continued almost without a break until the 30th. As the *Official History* says:

> By the middle of October conditions on and behind the battle-front were so bad as to make mere existence a severe trial of body and spirit. Little could be seen from the air through the rain and mist, so counter-battery work suffered and it was often impossible to locate with accuracy the new German trenches and shell-hole positions. Objectives could not always be identified from ground level, so that it is no matter for surprise or censure that the British artillery sometimes fired short or placed its barrages too far ahead. Bursts of high-explosive were smothered in the ooze; many guns had been continuously in action for over two months and were too worn for accurate fire; in some partially flooded battery positions sinking platforms had to be restored with any battle debris which came to hand. The ground was so deep in mud that, to move one 18-pounder, ten or twelve horses were often needed, and, to supplement the supplies brought by light railway and pack-horse, ammunition had to be dragged up on sledges improvised from sheets of corrugated iron. The infantry, sometimes wet to the skin and almost exhausted before Zero hour, were often condemned to struggle painfully forward through the mud under heavy fire against objectives vaguely defined and difficult of recognition.

These conditions made it almost impossible to make coherent plans for action. Orders were repeatedly issued, cancelled and replaced by fresh orders, only for these to be cancelled yet again.

On 3 November Holford-Walker sent to Lieutenant-Colonel Bradley, the Heavy Section commanding officer, a summary of reports submitted by the commanders of tanks in each group concerning the condition both of the ground and of the crossing points where the British trenches had been bridged or ramped to enable the tanks to pass.

A group: Out of five possible crossings two are damaged. The ground is very wet.

B group: Two crossings are damaged and the ground from Observation Wood to the front line is very bad and soft. Section commander reports this tank group cannot function owing to the terrible nature of the ground immediately behind our front line. He has in consequence been to 3rd Division whose views on the readjustment of this group will be forwarded as soon as received.

C group: Crossings reported in fairly good order. Ground very wet. Rob Roy Trench reported very badly damaged.

D group: As for C group.

E group: Crossings reported alright. Ground reported very wet and in three places very swampy.

F and G groups: Ground reported fair. Crossings good as far as Vallade Trench, i.e. the starting point. Our own front line and no-man's-land are reported in a very bad condition and very wet. No-man's-land is reported being full of shell holes filled with water.

On this same day, GHQ's OAD 199 endorsed the decision taken by Fifth Army the day before:

In view of the difficulties involved by constant postponements of the operations of the Fifth Army due to weather conditions, the GOC Fifth Army is now authorised to make an indefinite postponement of those operations, with the proviso that arrangements are made to bring on the attack without delay as soon as the weather shows signs of becoming more settled.

However, OAD 207 issued later the same day would seem to have contradicted the earlier instruction by announcing a specific date for further operations, albeit on a reduced scale:

The Fifth Army will make preparations forthwith for a limited attack to the line St Pierre Divion – Beaucourt – Serre to take place on Thursday next, 9th November, weather permitting. If the weather is suitable the Fifth Army will make a further bound as soon as possible thereafter.

On 6 November 3rd Division relayed a Reserve Army instruction to all the units under its command saying that, unless the weather improved very considerably, tanks would not be used. It did improve, but not by much – certainly not enough to dry out the ground to an extent enabling the tanks to advance without danger of capsizing in the mud. Even an infantry operation was now in doubt.

Several days were to pass before an attack – whether by tanks and infantry or infantry on their own – became once more a possibility. After much deliberation by G.H.Q., General Gough and his Corps Commanders, it was decided on 11 November to resume the offensive on the 13th. Even then the doubts lingered. Lieutenant-General Kiggell, Haig's Chief of Staff, called on Gough on the 12th and said that the Commander-in-Chief 'did not in any way wish to bring on a battle in unfavourable circumstances'. Haig himself joined the meeting later that same day, and questioned Gough further. Apparently satisfied that the gamble was worth it, he authorised the attack – putting into effect, on a reduced scale, the offensive planned several weeks earlier. The immediate objectives were the same Green and Yellow Lines as before, but any further progress towards the more distant Blue, Brown and Pink Lines was to depend on the weather.

All units were, of course, required to anticipate the go-ahead by preparing and issuing their orders for the attack. On 11 November Holford-Walker issued his own Operational Order no. 8 containing instructions for the role which the tanks were to play. They were to leave their places of assembly at 7 p.m. on Y/Z night and proceed straight to their start points. The laying of tapes to guide them across the British trenches and into no-man's-land was to be carried out between 5.30 and 7.30 p.m.

Leaving their start points at Zero, they were to accompany the infantry but not precede them, unless these were held up at any point. On arrival at the Yellow Line, and having seen the infantry firmly consolidated there, the tanks were to withdraw, those with 2nd Division making for K35a Central. This was just above the Quadrilateral (Heidenkopf) and on the road leading to Serre, where they would be ready no doubt to take part in any supporting action required of them further forward. The tanks with 3rd Division were to go to the hollow near Rob Roy Trench, and those with XIII Corps to behind Matthew Copse. On arrival at these points the tank commanders were to refill and await orders, first reporting to V Corps advance headquarters at the Lyceum[4] at K34a 5.5.

The positions of various other headquarters in the area were now changed to: Heavy Section (Lieutenant-Colonel Bradley) at the Lyceum, and C Company (Major Holford-Walker) at K34a 5.4 adjacent to it. Captain Clively remained at K28b 4½.1 but the headquarters of Captain Hiscocks seem to have been moved from Vallade Trench to White City (a chalkpit at Q4a 6.2). Meanwhile 3rd Division's headquarters remained at K28c 2.2 and those of 2nd Division at Q2b Central, this latter some distance to the rear, by the Sugar Factory.

At 6 p.m. on the evening of 11 November the tanks left Beaussart and made their way, probably via Colincamps, to the position of assembly in the lane by Jeremiah Trench south-west of La Signy Farm. All arrived safely but the journey, in almost complete darkness, was difficult. The ground was very soft and the tanks sank in badly. Where the ground was unbroken they could just about move, but where it had been shelled they could not. Lieutenant Bates ditched when near the Military Cemetery north-west of the Sugar Factory but managed to extricate himself. His problem was attributed to insufficient time spent on reconnaissance.

In the early morning of 12 November Holford-Walker told his superiors in V Corps that in his opinion the tanks could not function owing to the state of the ground. Consequently, he was ordered at noon to withdraw them all, and as soon as it was dark they headed back to Beaussart.

By 8.30 p.m. almost all had gone. The exceptions were one machine which had broken a track and three others which appear to have been at the tail-end of the column of tanks leaving the area and were still on the road leading from the Sugar Factory back to Colincamps. They were those of Lieutenants Clarke, Lambert and Reardon, these last two being recent arrivals in C Company. A hurried message was sent by Holford-Walker telling them to halt where they were, for at 8.30 p.m. he had been instructed to leave two machines back at Jeremiah Trench. The reason for this change of plan was disclosed at 11 p.m. when a further order told him to move two tanks to K27b 9.5 ready to support 31st Division in XIII Corps. Apparently the two which had earlier been allotted to the division (those of Captain Bennewith and Captain Lord Rodney) had been wrongly withdrawn from it, and were not now available to rejoin it in time for the opening of the battle the next day. These other two machines were therefore required to take their place under cover of darkness in order to assist the infantry when the battle opened. Note that Holford-Walker chose to keep back three tanks, not just two – a wise decision in the circumstances, for at some stage Clarke's tank became stuck fast in the mud.

At 5.45 a.m. on the 13th, an hour and a half before sunrise, the battle opened, most of C Company's tanks by now, of course, being far from the scene. Despite a massive artillery bombardment the infantry's progress was slow, being hampered by the mud, the shell-torn ground and the resolute stand of an enemy well established behind strong defences which he had occupied for many months past.

It is not the purpose of this book to describe in detail the infantry's efforts to break through those defences; suffice it to say that gallantry, skill and the expenditure of much blood by the British here were not enough, at least on this first day, to take them more than a few hundred metres beyond the Germans' front line. Certainly Beaumont Hamel was captured by the 51st Division further south but on 2nd Division's front only modest gains were made, and on 3rd Division's none at all.

The lack of progress during the day is probably why XIII Corps decided at 5 p.m. that the tanks which it had asked for would serve no purpose after all and should be withdrawn. Whether or not this was after further advice from Holford-Walker we do not know, but it must have been with a sigh of relief that he cancelled the arrangements he had made.

However, at 11 a.m. on 14 November he was warned that these same two tanks would be required to support a new, limited operation by 2nd Division. At a meeting held at the division's Advanced HQ at 1.30 p.m. he learned that

Map 11c. Miraumont.

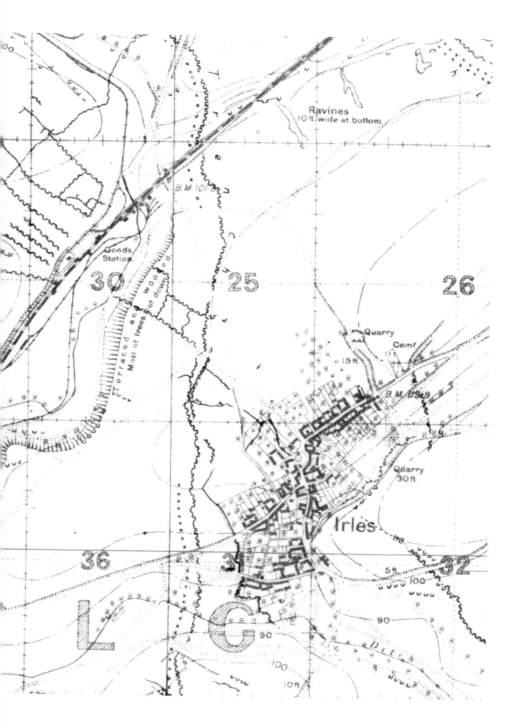

they were to attack the Quadrilateral in front of Serre at 6 a.m. on the following day, the 15th. Upon his return he told Captain Clively to make all the arrangements, and Captain Hiscocks to lay out the tapes guiding the tanks onto their objective.

The Quadrilateral (the Heidenkopf) was a most formidable strong-point, with massive defences dominating no-man's-land and the British lines beyond. It had caused countless casualties on 1 July and during the following four and a half months. Its capture was crucial to any advance in this sector. The risks to the tanks posed by the swampy ground leading up to it were clearly thought to be justified by the advantage which any success would confer on the accompanying infantry. Clively described the action in a report submitted to Holford-Walker later in the day:

> In pursuance of your order I sent 2/Lt R.G. Lambert and 2/Lt J. Reardon into action in the morning of 15th November 1916. The two tanks concerned moved off from Colincamps-Sucrerie Avenue at 2 a.m. and proceeded along the tape already laid. Ground was good over the tape and the tanks reached 6th Brigade HQ in Vallade Trench at 5 a.m., where I reported their arrival. I asked the G.O.C. to inform his battalion C.O.s that I had arrived, and would like them to send any information of value to my tank commanders by scout orderly to the tanks lying just west of Vallade Trench.
>
> By some accident my tanks never got any information at all from the battalions attacking.
>
> I gave orders for the tanks to proceed at 6 a.m. on a course slightly south of east as far as the enemy's front line, paying special attention to the enemy machine gun at K35c 40.85 which had been giving a lot of trouble to our infantry. After crossing the German front line [*they were*] to change course northward along Frontier Lane and assist the infantry in forming a defensive flank on the line K35a 9.2 and K35a 6.3. After consolidating, they were to return by the route followed in their advance.
>
> At 6 a.m. the tanks proceeded and were lost in the mist.
>
> I received a message at 8.15 a.m. that tank 744 (2/Lt Reardon) was stuck as per reference in his report [*not available*] and tank 523 (2/Lt Lambert) was also stuck at K34d 9.8. Later in the morning, all ranks reported to me at 6th Brigade HQ, having salved their guns and placed the tanks out of action.
>
> I attribute the fact of the tanks failing to gain their objective to the extraordinarily bad ground which they had to cross, which was worse than I imagined possible. The officers and men under my command did all humanly possible to get the tanks into a successful action and I would like to bring their efforts to your notice. As the tanks were under shell fire

and machine-gun fire from Serre, I decided to withdraw their crews and brought them back, without casualties, to the Point of [*illegible*] Avenue, Colincamps-Sucrerie.   Richard Clively, Capt Cmdg 4 Section

The tanks had been defeated not by the enemy but by the mud. Before writing his report Clively had already told Holford-Walker that 'tanks are stuck in No Man's Land, near Borden Avenue . . . absolutely ditched, mud coming up to the sponsons'.

This minor and unsuccessful action was all that C Company achieved in the sector north of Beaumont Hamel in the weeks before and during the British attack. Their next role in the drama was as bit-players assisting D Company south of the village.

Field Guide
IGN Map 2407O

To see the places associated with the movements of C Company's tanks at this time, it might be easiest to start with their approach route which ran near the Sugar Factory on the D919. Having come from Acheux and Beaussart, they must have approached this point either along the avenue of trees leading from Colincamps, or via Mailly-Maillet. The former beet-processing plant north of the road has now been replaced by a farmhouse and barns on its south side. Half a kilometre south-west of the farm is Auchonvillers Wood, where some of the tanks may have found shelter from enemy observation once they had entered this forward area. The name is a little confusing because the actual village of Auchonvillers, a kilometre further south, is on the route used by D Company.

Due west of La Signy Farm (written locally as Lassigny) was the track, still lined by trees, known as Jeremiah Road. This is part of the departmental boundary between the Pas de Calais and the Somme, and is where K27d 1.4 served as the main point of assembly for C Company's machines and where its main dump of stores was held. At K28c 2.2, 150m south-east of the farm, the advanced headquarters of 3rd Division housed those also of Major Allan Holford-Walker, though only for a limited period. Captain Clively's headquarters were near Observation Wood (unnamed on the IGN map), which lies 700m north-east of La Signy. Hiscocks' was at first to be co-located with the staff of 5th Infantry Brigade at K34b 0.1, housed in a dug-out in Vallade Trench. This important work crossed the D919 obliquely north-west/south-east, almost exactly in line with the departmental boundary about 400m west of the entrance to Serre Road British Cemetery No. 2. (Ignore the old marker-stone much nearer the cemetery. Ignore also the change of asphalt on the road nearby, which elsewhere is usually a sign of a departmental boundary.) The Lyceum was sited 300m further up Vallade, but is best reached by going up the track leading north just beyond the road junction at spot height 148 on the new IGN map, or 147 on older editions. It extends for 200m to a point where in 1916 it would have formed a T-junction with Cheeroh Avenue.

Serre Road No. 2 cemetery itself lies almost entirely in the no-man's-land of 1916 but the German defences just touched the easternmost corner, those of the British the western corner by the main road. A few metres outside the perimeter wall, at K35c 40.85, stood the German machine gun that was one of Second Lieutenant Reardon's targets. We do not know exactly where he became stuck, but in Lambert's case we do. K34d 9.8 lies about 40–50m outside the southwest-facing wall.

---

1   Matthew, Mark, Luke and John were four small clumps of trees opposite the German positions near Serre. It was from these that some of the British forces that suffered so cruelly on 1 July 1916 – notably some of the 'Pals' battalions – launched their ill-fated assault. Matthew Copse has now disappeared, and the others have been allowed to grow into one, now called Bois des Princesses.

2   A Fourth Army conference on 17 September was told that only eighteen qualified mechanics were available (IWM, Rawlinson Papers).

3   These tanks were different from the two destroyed by enemy shelling on 23 October on the Pozières–Courcelette road. See previous chapter.

4   The Lyceum is a theatre in London, long famous for the dramas enacted on its stage.

Chapter 12

Beaumont Hamel (South): October and November

On 16 October, the day after GHQ issued its order cancelling the earlier plans for an attack (see previous chapter), Major Frank Summers received a briefing on Haig's revised instructions and on the role envisaged for his D Company tanks. They were now to operate with the 63rd (Royal Naval) Division next to the Ancre and with the 51st (Highland) Division in Beaumont Hamel and the area to its immediate south. These, like their comrades in the 2nd and 3rd Divisions above the village, had several Objectives – the Green, Yellow, Blue and Red Lines extending eastwards from the German front line all the way across to Miraumont.

Wasting no time, Summers, accompanied by Captains Mortimore and Vandervell, set off during the afternoon of the 16th to go to Mesnil and Auchonvillers in order to reconnoitre possible start points and routes. The following evening each of these two officers conducted his own further survey, Mortimore going to Mesnil and Vandervell to Auchonvillers. Mortimore took with him some of his subalterns to help in the task but they all concluded that the routes available to them from Mesnil were unsuitable. A further reconnaissance, led again by Summers, agreed with their findings and the route via Auchonvillers was finally selected for all of D Company's tanks.

On the 19th officers spent time familiarising themselves with their allotted routes and discussing with Engineer officers the necessary preliminary work that was to be carried out, such as 'ramping' of the British trenches to enable the tanks to pass over them. This took the form either of re-filling a portion of trench long enough to take the width of a tank or, more often, using a device described in the War Diary of the 63rd Division as follows:

> Owing to the wet weather it was decided that some provision was necessary to assist our tanks across our trenches. Bridges were

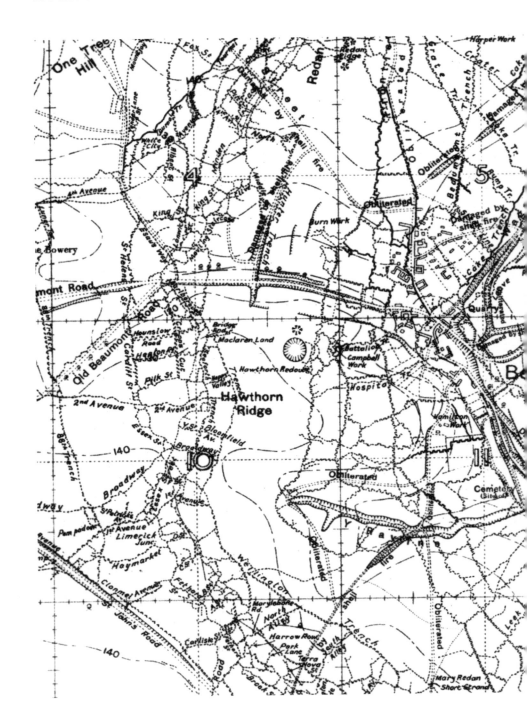

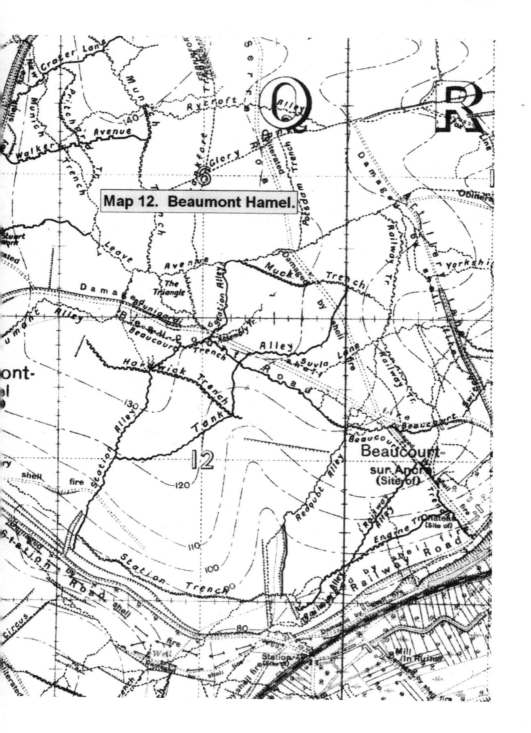

Map 12. Beaumont Hamel.

considered unnecessary, but planks 6' x 2' x 10ft [*15 x 5 x 300cms*] were laid parallel to the trench, spaced at 1ft [*30cms*] centres, the plank nearest the trench being 3ft [*90cms*] from the edge of the trench. Six planks each side were used, the intention being to distribute the load and prevent the trench from crushing in.[1]

On the 20th and 21st more time was spent in studying the routes and preparing maps of the ground to be crossed. Lieutenants Enoch and Huffam were despatched with a working party to prepare a dump for stores and a battle headquarters.

At 6 p.m. on 22 October (W/X night, Z Day being the 25th) D Company's tanks moved off from their base at Acheux *en route* to Beaussart, the 'half-way house' before Auchonvillers. Much time was spent here on the 23rd in overhauling the tanks and tuning the engines, but the rain which had earlier set in now began to threaten the whole operation, tanks and infantry alike. The ground became increasingly sodden and the mud increasingly deep under the tracks. It cannot have surprised anyone when that evening Summers announced to the crews that higher command had decided on a postponement of 48 hours, from the 25th to the 27th.

On the 25th a further postponement of 48 hours was announced, from the 27th to the 29th, and on the 28th most of the crews were withdrawn and returned to Acheux. The tanks were left where they were at Beaussart, with guards mounted around them. On the 29th Z Day was postponed to 5 November, and on 4 November it was postponed indefinitely. On the 6th Captain A.G. Woods, the D Company adjutant, left the area for the rear in order to prepare a winter base for the tanks and crews. His duties were taken over by Captain Mann.[2]

The rain fell continuously, it seems, until the 8th, but from the 9th onwards there was an improvement in the weather and the decision was taken to press ahead with the operation. At 6.30 p.m. on the 11th the tanks of D Company left Beaussart for Auchonvillers, where they arrived about midnight. The following day, the 12th, the tanks were given a final check, tapes up to the front line were laid and instructions were studied for the umpteenth time.

Then at 4 p.m. news was received that the tanks were not going to be used after all. This, according to the *Official History*, was because O.C. Tanks (either Lieutenant-Colonel Bradley or Major Summers) had warned V Corps that the bad state of the ground would prevent the machines from taking part. Summers was therefore directed to withdraw them at night. Accordingly the tapes were collected and the stores dump was prepared for removal. At 6.30 p.m. the tanks began the weary, forlorn trudge back to Beaussart, along roads and tracks now crowded with infantry who must have wondered why these ungainly monsters, upon which hopes were no doubt still pinned, were heading in the wrong direction.

However, at 11 p.m. the column was halted by Summers, who ordered two machines to return once more to Auchonvillers. It is probable that the two in question were chosen because they were last in the line wending its way back, and were thus less likely to cause chaos on the crowded road as they turned around. They were those of Lieutenants Bruce and Telfer, with Captain Vandervell in charge. The request for their return apparently emanated from 51st (Highland) Division, as we shall see, but for the time being they were required simply to stand by and await further orders.

At 5.45 a.m. on the 13th, an hour and a half before sunrise, the battle opened. Thousands of men heaved themselves over the parapet, then staggered forward over the shell-torn ground, slipping and sliding in the mud of no-man's-land, the way ahead illuminated only by the almost constant flash of the barrage falling on the German lines in front. Many men fell almost at once, their comrades unable to stop long enough to give them more than a pitying glance as they pressed on.

But in many places those survivors were themselves prevented from advancing very far by the withering fire of German machine guns and rifles. Companies lost their way in the darkness and mist and were soon without officers to lead them on.

It is not our task here to describe in detail the course of the battle. Much has been written about it elsewhere.[3] Our concern is more to discover what part D Company's tanks played in the unfolding struggle.

Their first involvement, indeed their only active involvement on this day, was that of Bruce and Telfer. At 9.50 a.m. Fifth Army headquarters suggested to V Corps that they could be used to help 'complete the capture of Beaumont Hamel if not already captured'. The commander of 51st Division, Major-General Sir Montagu Harper, readily accepted, and called on them to help break the German defences in and around the caves – some of them actually underground quarries – in the northern and south-eastern parts of the village. Alas, the two men, who had joined D Company only recently and had had no experience of tank fighting, were unable to progress very far. They advanced down the road from Auchonvillers until they reached a point, Q4d 95.15, just beyond the German front line. Here one of them is said to have ditched, either in the mud or perhaps in a shell hole made by British artillery pounding the enemy defences at an earlier stage of the battle. The other tank is said in one report to have reached a point north of the village and to have become stuck in mud there but we have been unable to discover precisely where.

During this same morning a message was sent to Captain Mortimore instructing him to leave Beaussart again for Auchonvillers with six tanks. Three only set out at 11.30 a.m. and arrived at their destination at 3.05 p.m. but this was too late to take part in this first day of fighting.[4] Their recall was in direct response to an appeal from Major-General Shute, of 63rd (Royal Naval)

Division. From the outset of the British attack, an isolated strong-point said to be about Q17b 7.4 had caused great trouble to the troops of this division fighting on the right flank, next to the Ancre. Hideous casualties were suffered by Hawke and Nelson Battalions in the right centre, by Howe and Anson Battalions in the left centre, and by both Royal Marine Battalions on the left. Arrangements were made for Mortimore's three tanks to be sent early in the morning of the 14th to attack this strong-point, Lieutenants H.C.F. Drader and F.A. Robinson being detailed for the task, with Lieutenant Bell's tank following in reserve.

On the journey up to the start point Robinson's tank was hit by shell fire and put out of action. In the dark and in the mist it can only have been a chance shot – but for the Germans a lucky one – to have landed where it did.

The two remaining tanks set off from their start point at Zero, 6 a.m., probably with Drader in the lead. He took on board a guide, a trench mortar officer named Lieutenant Allan Campbell RNVR, who had already reconnoitred the approaches to the German lines and was now able to direct the tanks towards their objective. Once into no-man's-land they still had to make their way as best they could through the myriad shell-holes which lay everywhere about them, but by now it was getting light and Campbell was able, through the mist, to see where the strong-point lay. Drader took the machine across the German front line and aimed for the second line whence soon came streams of machine-gun bullets which confirmed the place as their target. Drader now opened fire with his 6-pounders, sending round after round into the area of the dug-outs.

Suddenly, disaster. The tank ditched and became stuck fast in the mud.

Almost immediately Bell's tank, which had not yet crossed the German first line, also ditched, but both tanks continued firing at the target, Bell from further back, still in no-man's-land, his fire guided by the visible impact of Drader's rounds.

But then, a wholly unexpected sight. The ground in front of Drader seemed to be shimmering with white:

> On opening the front flap of the tank and obtaining a better view, it was seen that all the German garrison, some four hundred in number, appeared to have found something white to wave in token of surrender; those who could not produce anything better were waving lumps of white chalk about or bits of board or rifle stocks which they had rapidly chalked white. The situation was rather an embarrassing one for so small a number as the crew of two tanks to deal with; fortunately, however, it was possible by signs, and with the assistance of the infantry, to mop up these four hundred prisoners before they realised that both the tanks were stuck and out of action.

Drader's account seems unduly modest. The War Diaries put it this way:

> At 50 yards range Lieutenant Drader opened fire with 6-pdr guns. The tanks still advanced and crossed the first line of the strong-point doing good enfilade work. Simultaneously the enemy hoisted the white flag. Both tanks at this moment became ditched and an awkward situation arose, which was handled splendidly by both officers. A machine gunner was detailed to look for any sign of treachery on the part of the enemy, and the officers and crews then left the tanks and entered the German trenches. With loaded revolvers they coaxed the enemy out of their dug-outs and after about an hour the prisoners who numbered over 400 were despatched to the rear with an infantry escort.

So, unless the War Diary has embellished the facts, it seems likely that both Drader and Bell entered the German trenches themselves before British infantry arrived on the scene to help. The diarist later wrote:

> When the adverse conditions as regards ground are reckoned with, this must be considered a very fine performance and all ranks are to be congratulated.

Describing the initial advance, Major-General Shute later wrote;

> Considerable casualties were caused by machine-gun fire from a cunningly concealed strong-point which afterwards proved to be in the centre of the portion of the enemy's position, opposite the Division's front, and the emplacements of which had not been completely destroyed by our artillery fire . . . On approaching the German system, though close under our barrage, the Hawke Battalion, followed by the Nelson Battalion, came under very heavy machine-gun fire from the strong-point. The Commanding Officer of the Hawke Battalion, three company commanders and many other officers became casualties, and the battalion lost so heavily that only small parties reached the third line. The Nelson Battalion also suffered heavily from this fire, and by the time it had reached the third line it had lost nearly all its officers, and was far behind the barrage . . . On the left and left centre 1st Royal Marines and the Howe Battalion, with 2nd Royal Marines and Anson Battalion behind them, were also hung up, after passing the front line, by machine-gun fire from the strong-point on their right . . . Here the attack, with the exception of small parties, did not succeed in penetrating beyond the German second line for some considerable time, and in some places did not penetrate beyond the front line. A large proportion of company commanders were killed or wounded.
>
> The strong-point was built in the form of a single communication trench, and from this cause its presence had not been disclosed by aeroplane photographs beforehand. The dug-outs which it contained

were very deep, and three concrete machine-gun emplacements, approached by ladders from the dug-outs, had been quite untouched by our bombardments. It would appear that these machine guns were able to fire continuously in spite of our barrage, and that the trench in which the dug-outs were situated was never entered by our leading waves. Several other dug-outs, however, were probably missed in the fog by the cleaning up waves, which accounted for the presence of Germans in other parts of the front system.

Clearly the threat which this emplacement posed to the British advance was of a most serious order, so Shute, now painfully aware of this, had turned to the tanks for help.

I asked permission from Corps HQ to make use of my six tanks at Auchonvillers, but was informed that they had been ordered back to Beaussart the night before. However, I arranged that three of them should at once be brought back to Auchonvillers, but this required so much time that I could only arrange that they should come into action against the strong-point at daybreak on the 14th, if it were not previously captured. The 188th Infantry Brigade was at the same time ordered to detail an officer to reconnoitre a route, and to guide the tanks into the strong-point.

The three tanks approached our lines from Auchonvillers during the night, and arrived at the rendezvous an hour before dawn. Here they were met by Lieutenant Allan Campbell RNVR, who . . . got into the leading tank which he then steered towards the enemy's line. Just before starting, hostile shells fell in the neighbourhood of the tanks, one of which was knocked out, but as it was still dark, and as there was a thick mist, it is practically certain that these were merely chance shots. The remaining two tanks crossed into no-man's-land successfully but found the ground very muddy, and turned southwards along no-man's-land in the hope of finding a better place for crossing the enemy's front line trench. One tank then crossed half-way between the Germans' first and second lines, where it stuck. The other tank also stuck, on our side of the German line. Both tanks then came into action with their 6-pounders, and the Germans immediately raised the white flag. However, as there was some delay in the Germans coming out to surrender, the crews of the tanks got out of their machines with their Hotchkiss guns and advanced along the trench towards the enemy. Thereupon the enemy at once surrendered and two officers and some 400 men were taken prisoners.

Thus the strong-point, which had successfully prevented our completing the capture of the enemy second line, was now captured, but there were still a number of Germans and machine guns in their old third line. It was evident, however, that these men were only awaiting an opportunity to surrender.

And surrender they did. One report puts a total at 600, including six officers, taken from dug-outs under an embankment.[5] Others quote a figure of 500 for the two locations.[6]

The significance of the tanks' role in this operation should not be underestimated. The guns in the strong-point had caused hundreds of casualties in the advancing British ranks on the 13th and 14th, and would have been capable of inflicting many more had the tanks not arrived on the scene. Said the Hawke diarist:

> The battalion, after the first few minutes of the attack, no longer existed as a unit. It transpired later that we attacked immediately in front of a very strong German redoubt. The battalion suffered grievous losses. It is known that, in the first few minutes, and in front of this redoubt, the colonel, adjutant and three company commanders became casualties.
>
> After it was relieved, members of the battalion went back to the enemy strong-point which had caused so much trouble. This had been captured in the morning of the 14th by two tanks. This redoubt was a marvellous piece of work and should have been able to hold out very much longer. The appearance of the tanks, however, so terrified the Germans that they instantly surrendered. Frequent tunnels ran out from it into no-man's-land, having skilfully constructed machine-gun emplacements and sniper posts.

The diary of 10th Royal Dublin Fusiliers tells us that the strong-point:

> extended from the German front trench to their Reserve trench and had four entrances in front and two each in the Support and Reserve Lines. This dug-out was capable of taking 1,500 men. It had electric plant installed, and ammunition stocks and was evidently used to reinforce the different lines, as well as being an Aid Station. The Boche had machine guns covering each entrance, and various snipers in between. Two of the entrances in the first line were subsequently bombed by two bombing parties led by Second Lieutenants McMahon and Cox and the occupants surrendered.

That the infantry who arrived on the scene some time after the tanks should have found some opposition still remaining shows how dangerous a task was undertaken by both Drader and Bell in tackling the garrison alone. Clearly the Germans regarded this emplacement as a key feature of their defences in this sector. It certainly took a heavy toll of the British, whose wounded, dead and dying were left in swathes over the slopes below. To take just a few examples, the 1st Royal Marines went into battle 480 strong. Only 138 fit men returned – fit, but exhausted. No fewer than 47 of their comrades had been killed, 210 wounded, and 85 were missing. Of the 22 officers who took part, only 2 survived unscathed; 6 had been killed, 11 had been wounded and 3 were missing. Over the period 13–15 November, Drake Battalion lost 6 of its officers killed, including the Commanding Officer, Lieutenant-Colonel A.S. Tetley, and 7 wounded. 15 Other Ranks were killed, 151 wounded, and 28 were missing.

The fact that the strong-point was said to have had several entrances, including those facing the British, explains why reports from the infantry had given several different map references for its position. It was variously said to be at Q17b 8.2, 9.4, 7.4 and 7.2.

An interesting light has recently been thrown on the construction of this underground complex. Lining the north-eastern face of the ridge, hidden from British view, lay Kolonie, a seemingly innocent row of huts 'looking for all the world like a navvies' encampment'. A photograph taken in June 1916 shows these with their backs to the higher ground, and it was through these huts that tunnels were dug into the rising slope, thereafter branching out into the chambers which so impressed the British troops who eventually searched them once the occupants had surrendered to Drader and Bell. The tunnels then penetrated to the surface on the south-western flank of the ridge where they formed excellent machine-gun nests – no doubt the 'entrances' facing the British.[7]

It was clearly as a result of the tanks' success in eliminating this major obstacle that later, at 3 p.m., orders were received to move six machines further forward – apparently now including reinforcements from Beaussart – under the command of Captain G. Nixon, and to take up position near Beaucourt Station. Their route was to take them over the cratered wastes of no-man's-land, then across the original German front trenches. There were no tracks or roads to follow, so Captain Mann was instructed to find a suitable route and, with 150 men, to build a properly defined path for the tanks to follow.

But at 5 p.m. this forward movement was postponed. Mortimore and Vandervell, together with the officers and crews who had been in action, then left the area, leaving Captain Nixon in command under Major Summers.

Little happened on the 15th, but on the 16th Summers himself conducted a reconnaissance of the ground leading to Beaucourt Station. When he returned to his headquarters he was met by Colonel Bradley, who confirmed that he should resume the tanks' forward movement to the station. At 6 p.m. they moved off, but the going was so bad that they all became ditched on the way. The whole of the 17th was spent in digging them out and making them operational once more.

But one of them was made ready fairly quickly and its commander, Second Lieutenant Walter Partington, was instructed to take it forward without delay, up to the place of assembly at Q12 Central – a point close to a trench later called Tank Alley. His orders were that on the 18th he should at zero, proceed north to cross Beaucourt Trench near its junction with Frankfort Trench. Continue along Frankfort Trench to Leave Alley. When position is consolidated, return by same route and park tank in the Ravine near Beaucourt Station.

These orders fail to make it clear that the actual target was the Triangle, a strong-point immediately north of the Beaumont–Beaucourt road, its eastern side apparently being regarded as part of Frankfort Trench and its northern side being Leave Avenue (rather than Alley). It was here that men of 37th Division, coming from the south, were supposed to bring flanking fire to bear on Germans being driven back by an attack from the west by 32nd Division – a plan frustrated by the Germans' success in stemming the advance of the latter. Partington's instructions make it fairly clear that Leave Avenue was as far as he was to go.

At what point he arrived on the scene we do not know but it would appear that, seeing the failure of 32nd Division to break into and through the Munich and Frankfort Trenches, and the consequent inability of 37th Division to assist in ejecting the enemy from this area, Partington decided to press ahead north of the Triangle in order to come up behind those trenches and attack their occupants from the east. The diarist later wrote:

> Lieutenant Partington carried out orders as detailed. The tank crossed the junction of Beaucourt and Frankfort Trenches at 6.45 a.m. From thence onwards his guns were firing continuously, causing great havoc amongst the enemy. At one period he was attacked by a party of about thirty bombers. The port guns successfully dealt with them and none escaped. A train of twenty-five pack mules was observed at about 400 yards range, and put out of action with machine-gun fire. Many machine guns were encountered and dealt with. The British infantry did not advance during these manoeuvres, so at 9.07 a.m. Lieutenant Partington crossed Beaucourt Trench and returned to the Ravine. Casualties were two ORs wounded.

In fact, Partington had done more than this citation claimed. A report from observers in 37th Division watching from the opposite bank of the Ancre said that his tank had got as far as Q6b 2.4, a point well up the Beaucourt–Serre road and beyond Glory Lane, where it was being heavily shelled, despite being close up against the rear of the German defenders in Frankfort Trench.[8]

Here he must have realised that he and his crew were not going to win this battle totally on their own so he turned about. The same observers who had seen him go north now reported that at 8.55 a.m. his machine had come back down the road to Q6d 7.3 and was now moving along Muck Trench in a south-easterly direction. Individual men could be seen moving with it but these must have been men of 37th Division escorting it back to their positions.

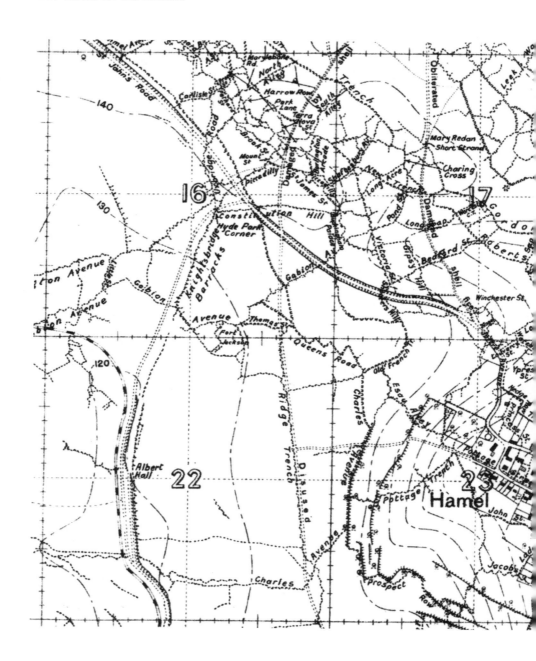

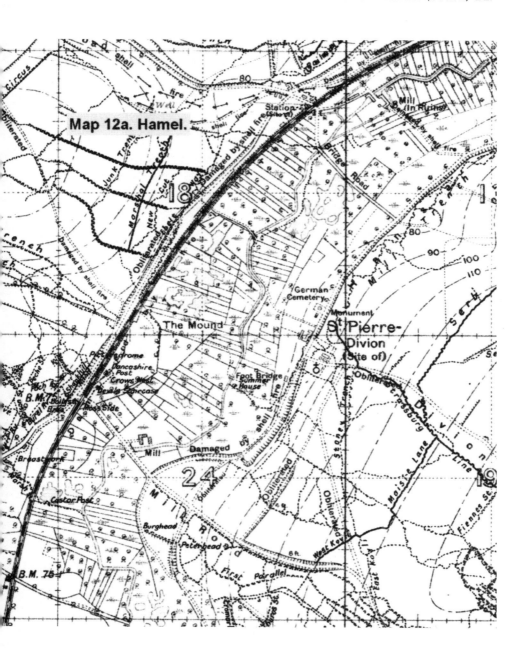

Map 12a. Hamel.

Thereafter he almost certainly kept to a route alongside Tank Alley.

For his action on this day, Partington was awarded (oddly, one might think) the Italian Silver Medal,[9] the citation reading:

> He commanded an isolated tank in action on the morning of 18th November 1916. He remained in action for two hours under close fire from machine guns, trench mortars and bombers, out of touch with our own troops, and inflicted losses on the enemy. He continued to fight his tank after two of the crew were wounded, and only returned to our lines in order to undertake a fresh attack in cooperation with the infantry.

But he did not attack again. He and his men were now utterly exhausted, and incapable of further effort. We have to remember, however, that their undoubtedly brave actions might not have been possible had it not been for the part played in the enterprise by an Intelligence Officer working with the Heavy Section, Capt Frederick Elliott Hotblack MC. He took it upon himself not simply to guide the tank to its target by laying tapes out along the first part of its route but also, when these had been covered by snow, by actually leading the tank forward by walking in front of it, despite the hail of enemy bullets aimed at the tank – and therefore at him. He may not have accompanied Partington all the way but he clearly deserved his DSO:

> For conspicuous gallantry in action on 18th November 1916. A tank being halted from uncertainty as to the proper direction, this officer went forward on foot through very heavy fire and guided the tank to its objective by walking in front of it. He displayed great courage and determination throughout.

There is no other reference that we have seen to Partington's 'uncertainty' as to his direction. He obviously displayed none when he pressed forward, behind the German lines, but whether this was due to his own determination or to Hotblack's guidance is something that we shall never know.

Field Guide
IGN Map 2407EO

The place where the tank – that of either Bruce or Telfer – was brought to a halt outside the village of Beaumont Hamel was on the road leading into it from Auchonvillers, just east of where a rough path leads up to Hawthorn Crater.

To see the position of the redoubt captured by Drader and Bell, park your car outside the Ancre British Cemetery on the Hamel–Beaucourt road and walk up the steep, narrow road beside it. The asphalt ends after 260m, just short of the first trees. The German front line began at 400m, which is 20m before the track begins to bend right. At 510m Q17b 8.2 lies on your left, one of the reported machine-gun emplacements. Another was at Q17b 7.2, 50m further into the field. The field of fire here was superb. The principal entrance was probably at Q17b 9.4, on the east side of the track.

When you return to the main road, spare some time to visit the cemetery, where many of the men struck down by the guns of the redoubt lie buried.

Walter Partington set out on his solo journey, initially with Hotblack as his guide, from the 'ravine' opposite Beaucourt railway station (shown as Beaumont Hamel Station on the IGN map). This feature – less dramatic than the word implies – runs due north but is difficult to see from here owing to the buildings now bordering the road,[10] so drive into Beaucourt village and take the first turning left. A short distance up this narrow, one-way road a track leads left and gives a view into the ravine, should you wish to see this. Otherwise continue on up until you reach an oblique crossroads where you should bear left along the D163. Carry on, up to spot height 135, where a farm track comes up from the south, and the Triangle is immediately to the north. Now return to the crossroads and take the turning which leads you half-back to the left. At a point 50m short of where the power lines cross the road is where Muck Trench lay. After another 130m Leave Avenue crosses the road near the bend (spot height 128 on older IGN maps). Continue on, past the track on the right at spot height 130, to the place where a field boundary comes in from the left. Here you are on Glory Lane. As you round the next gentle bend, Q6b 2.4 lies about 100m into the field on your left, almost as far ahead as Rycroft Alley. This is where Partington turned his tank round at the end of his long, lone advance. One supposes that, throughout it, he had kept close to Frankfort Trench all the way from the Triangle, shooting into the rear of the enemy positions facing 32nd Division attacking from the west.

---

1   It was, of course, impossible to use this device to cross trenches on the other side of no-man's-land. It was not until November 1917, at the Battle of Cambrai, that 'fascines' – tightly bound bundles of wooden branches – were carried on the roofs of tanks and dropped into the enemy trenches as each machine approached the parapet. These enabled the tanks to cross trenches which by then the Germans had built wider than those of 1916.

2   The Author is grateful to Captain Graham Woods for the manner in which he maintained D Company's records. By no means perfect, they are nonetheless more detailed than those of other companies.

3   See for instance Nigel Cave's *Beaumont Hamel* in the Battleground Europe series.

4   According to the *Official History* some tanks 'had to be left in their forward positions' the evening before the battle, implying that this was due to the congestion which it says was on the roads leading up to the front, but there is evidence in several War Diaries not only that Bruce and Telford were called back after they had set out for Beaussart but also that Mortimore and his section of half a dozen tanks.were ordered back to Auchonvillers well after they had arrived at

Beaussart.

5   Statement in War Diary of Colonel Freyburg's Hood Battalion.

6   Statement in War Diary of 188th Infantry Brigade.

7   See Jack Sheldon, *The Germans at Beaumont Hamel* (Pen & Sword Books), p. 135.

8   We assume that these observers had telescopes and judged Partington's position here accurately, even though to see it they would have had to be on the high ground by the Schwaben Redoubt, 3km away.

9   It was a common practice in the First World War for Allied governments to hand out their medals to men of other armies. Partington was awarded the MC for a separate action in June 1918.

10 The word 'ravine' seems sometimes to have been applied to the whole of the valley between the river and Beaumont Hamel, and could equally well be applied to the narrow defile leading north from a point half-way along this, but on balance we think it must refer to the feature identified in our text.

Index